WHEN IN January 1649 the English Parliament ordered the trial and execution of its King, Charles Stuart, the event caused widespread amazement both in the kingdom and abroad. For kings were thought to rule by divine right, and their subjects were expected to obey them without question. Rebellion was not only high treason, but a blasphemy as well.

Why was Charles I executed by his subjects? Was this the cold-blooded murder of an innocent man, or did he bring death upon himself? What were the highlights of his trial in the ancient Westminster Hall, and what was the feeling of the crowds when he was publicly beheaded on a scaffold outside Whitehall Palace? Dr. Cowie draws on many key documents to suggest answers to these and other questions. He shows how the causes of the crisis must be traced back in English history a hundred years before. The problems faced by the monarchy, and the grievances expressed by Parliament, were already in evidence in Tudor times. To this difficult background were later added the unfortunate personalities of James I and Charles I, the outbreak of civil war, and the failure of the King and his opponents to agree on how to govern in future. Dr. Cowie shows how schemes and accidents, passions and ideals worked upon each other to produce the final act in the drama. Here is a uniquely exciting study of an event of deep significance for English history.

The Trial and Execution of Charles I

Leonard W. Cowie

WAYLAND PUBLISHERS · LONDON
G. P. PUTNAM'S SONS · NEW YORK

The Documentary History Series

MEDIEVAL PILGRIMS   *Alan Kendall*
THE REFORMATION OF THE SIXTEENTH CENTURY   *L. W. Cowie*
WITCHCRAFT   *Roger Hart*
THE PILGRIM FATHERS   *L. W. Cowie*
PLAGUE AND FIRE   *L. W. Cowie*
THE AGE OF DICKENS   *Patrick Rooke*
THE ORIGINS OF WORLD WAR ONE   *Roger Parkinson*
THE THIRD REICH   *Michael Berwick*
THE ORIGINS OF WORLD WAR TWO   *Roger Parkinson*
HIROSHIMA   *Marion Yass*
THE VIKINGS   *Michael Gibson*
THE BLACK DEATH AND PEASANTS' REVOLT   *L. W. Cowie*
ENGLAND EXPECTS   *Roger Hart*
THE COLD WAR   *Elisabeth Barker*
RUSSIA UNDER STALIN   *Michael Gibson*
BLACK CARGO   *Richard Howard*

Frontispiece The execution of Charles I

SBN (England): 85340 044 X
SBN (United States): 399-11035-6

Filmset in England in "Monophoto" Times by Keyspools Ltd,
Golborne, Lancashire. Printed in England by C. Tinling & Co. Ltd,
London and Prescot.

Contents

The Illustrations

Prologue

BY EARLY MORNING on Tuesday 30th January, 1649, an enormous gaping crowd of Londoners was pressed together outside the Banqueting House of Whitehall Palace. Before them rose a scaffold, which the carpenters had only just finished building. On it two executioners stood waiting, disguised in masks, false beards and wigs. Close at hand were iron chains and ropes to allow force which would be used if the prisoner tried to resist his fate. *A day of death*

After many hours of waiting, Charles Stuart, King of England was led up the steps to the scaffold. By his side was William Juxon, the Bishop of London. After making a short speech protesting his innocence, the royal prisoner stretched out his neck on the block. The axe swung down and severed the head from the body.

A boy who witnessed the grim scene afterwards wrote, "There was such a groan by the thousands there present as I never heard before, and desire I may never hear again."

*　　*　　*

To the people of Stuart England the trial and execution of Charles I was an amazing event. In seventeenth-century Europe every major country was a monarchy; kingship was thought to be decreed by God for the nations of mankind. For a king to be put to death by his subjects seemed to many a blasphemous crime.

Shortly before the trial a Royalist wrote in a secret pamphlet: "Never was such damnable doctrine vented before in the world, for the persons of sovereign princes have ever been held sacred ... even among the most barbarous nations. And though in many kingdoms they have been regulated by force of arms and sometimes ... deposed and afterwards privately murdered, yet in no *A damnable doctrine*

9

Opposite King Charles I of England

The scene in Whitehall as Charles I hands his watch to William Juxon, Bishop of London, just before his execution

history can we find a parallel for this, that ever the rage of rebels extended so far to bring their sovereign lord to public trial and execution, it being contrary to the law of nature, the custom of nations, and the sacred scriptures . . .

"What court shall their king be tried in? Who shall be his peers? Who shall give sentence? What eyes dare be so impious to behold the execution? What arm be stretched out to give the stroke against the Lord's Anointed, and shall not wither like that of Jeroboam, when he lifted it up against an anointed prophet? (1)"

Charles's faults   Later, when the event had become a matter of history, people began to think more calmly about it and question why it had happened. Gilbert Burnet, a Scotsman who became Bishop of Salisbury, thought that Charles I had brought down his fate upon himself. He pointed to his lack of judgment and good policy: "His reign, both in peace and war, was a continual series of errors, so that his judgment could hardly be good. He was

10

out of measure set upon following his own humour, but was unreasonably feeble to those he trusted. His notion of regal power was carried too high, and every opposition to it he thought rebellion. He minded little things too much, and was more concerned in drawing a paper than in fighting a battle.

"He had a firm aversion to Popery, but was much inclined to a middle way between Protestants and Papists, whereby he lost the one, without gaining the other (2)."

There was truth in this. In many ways Charles Stuart was poorly fitted to meet the testing years of his reign, and it has been said that "the King was his own executioner". But there is more to it than that. Charles's reign (1625–49) was a time of dispute about religion and politics which had begun years before he mounted the throne. Men held opposing beliefs and sought opposing aims. Those who killed the King believed that their deed would, as one of them said, "Live and remain upon record to the perpetual honour of the English state, who took no dark or doubtful way, no indirect by-course, but went in the open and plain path of Justice, Reason, Law and Religion (3)."

Charles's death justified

Men on both sides held high ideals which drove them to violence when the crisis came. Step by step, controversy and dispute led to civil war, and this did not settle the issue. War was followed by intrigue and further war, and the last act of violence was the death of the King. The regicides believed to the end that the deed had been done according to the will of God.

One of them, Thomas Harrison, said at his own trial years later: "I do not come to be denying anything, but rather to be bringing it forth to the light . . . It was not a thing done in a corner. I believe the sound of it hath been in most nations. I believe the hearts of some have felt the terrors of that presence of God that was with his servants in those days . . . I followed not my own judgment; I did what I did, as out of conscience to the Lord . . . Maybe I might be a little mistaken, but I did it all according to the best of my understanding, desiring to take the revealed will of God in his Holy Scriptures as a guide to me (4)."

Unrepentant regicide

Such men believed that they saw the hand of God in history. Only in the history of the years before Charles I's execution can the causes of it be seen and understood by us.

11

King Henry the eyght.

1 The Gathering Conflict

IN 1547, nearly a hundred years before the execution of Charles I, the famous Tudor monarch Henry VIII died. He had brought England safely through the Reformation, the greatest revolution in her history; he had transferred the authority once exercised by the Pope in England to the king, making the monarchy stronger than ever before. In a changing world, men clung to the protection of royal authority. England was the only state to undergo the Reformation without war in the sixteenth century; to the Tudors civil strife and disorder seemed an ever-present danger to be averted only by a strong monarchy.

Early in the next reign, the government issued some homilies to be read out by the clergy in church. One of them was the *Homily on Obedience*: "Almighty God hath created and appointed all things in heaven, earth and waters in a most excellent and perfect order. In heaven he hath appointed distinct orders and states of archangels and angels. In the earth he has assigned kings, princes, with other governors under them, all in good and necessary order . . . Every degree of people, in their vocation, calling and office, has appointed to them their duty and order. Some are in high degree, some in low; some kings and princes, some inferiors and subjects, priests and laymen, masters and servants, fathers and children, husbands and wives, rich and poor . . .

"Where there is no right order there reigneth all abuse, carnal liberty, enormity, sin, and Babylonical confusion. Take away kings, princes, rulers, magistrates, judges, and such states of God's order, no man shall ride or go by the highway unrobbed, no man shall sleep in his own house or bed unkilled, no man shall keep his wife, children and possessions in quietness; all things shall be common and there must needs follow all mischief and utter destruction . . . (5)"

Opposite Henry VIII in Parliament. He persuaded them to acquiesce to his break with the church in Rome

13

The homily emphasized that obedience was due to the king because he had been appointed by God to rule over his people. This belief was to play an important part in the troubled years before Charles I's execution: "God has sent us his high gift, our most dear sovereign lord, King Edward VI, with godly, wise and honourable council, with other superiors and inferiors, in a beautiful order. Wherefore let us subjects do our bounden duty . . . Let us all obey, even from the bottom of our hearts, all their godly proceedings, laws, statutes, proclamations and injunctions . . . Let us mark well and remember that the high power and authority of kings, with their making of laws, judgments and officers, are the ordinances not of man but of God . . . We may not resist, nor in any wise hurt, an anointed king which is God's lieutenant, vicegerent and highest minister in that country where he is king . . . (6)"

God's anointed king

The homily also foreshadowed the future by utterly condemning rebellion against the divinely-ordained authority of the king: "Yet let us believe undoubtedly, good Christian people, that we may not obey kings, magistrates or any other (though they be our own fathers) if they would command us to do anything contrary to God's commandments. In such a case we ought to say with the Apostles: we must rather obey God than man.

The vice of rebellion

"But nevertheless in that case we may not in any wise resist violently or rebel against rulers or make any insurrection, sedition or tumults, either by force of arms or otherwise, against the anointed of the Lord or any of his appointed officers. But we must in such cases patiently suffer all wrongs or injuries, referring the judgment of our case only to God . . .

"Let us all therefore fear the most detestable vice of rebellion, ever knowing and remembering that he that resisteth common authority resisteth God and His ordinance (7)."

The English Reformation brought about many changes in religion, but it was not intended to tolerate those who held individual views. Religious unity was thought to be as important as political unity. Everyone was expected to conform to the Church of England. The Act of Uniformity, passed by Parliament early in the reign of Queen Elizabeth I (1558–1603), insisted that all clergy were to "say and use the Matins, Evensong, celebration

Religious uniformity

15

Opposite Queen Elizabeth I (1558–1603)

Thomas Cranmer, Archbishop of Canterbury, being burnt at the stake
for his refusal to comply with Mary Tudor's religious policy

of the Lord's Supper, and the administration of the sacraments,
and all their common and open prayer, in such order and form as
is mentioned in the Book [of Common Prayer] so authorized by
Parliament (8)."

Heavy penalties Anyone who disobeyed the Act of Uniformity faced heavy
penalties. Even criticism of the Book of Common Prayer was
punished. Any clergyman who "shall preach, declare or speak
anything in the derogation or depraving of the said book . . . and
shall be [convicted] by verdict of twelve men or by his own
confession or by the notorious evidence of the fact, shall [forfeit]
for his first offence the profit of all his spiritual benefices or pro-
motions coming or arising in one whole year next after his
conviction [and] suffer imprisonment by the space of six months
without bail (9)."

Puritans But as time passed, many people began to think that the
Church of England was not properly reformed. They wanted
to "purify" it by making the clergy and people observe higher
standards of piety and morality; they wanted to make it more
like the Protestant Churches on the Continent in matters of
worship and government.

As Lucy Hutchinson explained in the biography of her
husband, this made them unpopular, and brought them the
nickname of "Puritans": "God in his mercy sent his prophets

16

Opposite A preacher with his congregation at St. Paul's Cross in the time
of James I

The Chancellors
Seat

into all corners of the land, to preach repentance, and cry out against the ingratitude of England, who thus requited so many rich mercies that no nation could ever boast of more . . . By these, a few were everywhere converted and established in faith and holiness. But at court they were hated, disgraced, and reviled, and in scorn had the name of Puritan fixed upon them (10)."

Among other things, the Puritans wanted laymen to share the duties of the parish clergy. In 1585 some of them asked Queen Elizabeth for "associates" — "four, six or eight inhabitants of his parish [to] govern his said parish with him; to hear and order with him such quarrels, offences, and disorders in life and manners, as should be among the same parishioners. And if the causes and quarrels . . . be such that the same pastor and his associates or seniors cannot determine the same [the pastor shall] bring the said cause before the bishop of the diocese and the elders, which are to him associate (11)." *Puritan demands*

Elizabeth would not listen to such views. She disliked religious argument because it made for disunity and disorder in the state. She was unwilling to make changes in the Church, and Puritans were prosecuted for defying the Act of Uniformity.

When some were put on trial in 1586 they put forward their demands with a defiance that boded ill for the religious peace of the kingdom. They demanded "that the worship of the English Church is flat idolatry: that we admit into our Church persons unsanctified: that our preachers have no lawful calling: that our government is ungodly: that no bishop or preacher preacheth Christ sincerely and truly: that the people of every parish ought to choose their bishop, and that every elder, though he be no doctor nor pastor, is a bishop: that all the precise which refuse the ceremonies of the Church and yet preach in the same Church, strain a gnat and swallow a camel and are close hypocrites and walk in a left-handed policy . . . that set prayer is blasphemous (12)." *Defiant Puritans*

Since Elizabeth would not listen to them, they tried to get the changes they wanted through Parliament. But the Queen did her best to have them silenced. As early as 1572, the records of the House of Commons (which had some Puritan members) stated: "Upon declaration made unto this house by Mr. Speaker from *Parliament silenced*

Opposite Queen Elizabeth I sitting in Parliament. The Commons stand at the bar at the back of the chamber

the Queen's majesty, that her highness' pleasure is that from henceforth no bills concerning religion shall be preferred or received into this house, unless the same should be first considered and liked by the clergy (13)."

The Puritans in Parliament were mostly Presbyterians. They wanted to model the Church on the teaching of the Swiss reformer, John Calvin (1509–64), as had already been done in Scotland. But there were also Independents who disliked an organized Church and believed that every congregation should be independent.

Presbyterians and Independents

Opposite This satirical view of a Presbyterian synod shows the suspicion with which many people regarded them

Below John Calvin, the Swiss reformer, on whose teachings Presbyterians based their doctrine

PROMPTE ET SINCERE ·

Some Independents began to hold their own services, and in 1593 Parliament passed an act against them: "If any person or persons [shall] willingly join or be present at any such assemblies, conventicles, or meetings [then] every such person so offending as aforesaid . . . shall be committed to prison, there to remain without bail or mainprise until they shall conform and yield themselves to come to some church, chapel, or usual place of common prayer and hear divine service according to her majesty's laws . . . (14)"

"Sweet is liberty" In this way religion and politics became bound up together, and already some people were challenging the way the Queen used her powers. In 1576 Peter Wentworth, a Puritan, was suspended from the House of Commons for uttering words disliked by the Queen. He said: "Mr. Speaker, I find written in a little volume these words in effect: 'Sweet is the name of liberty, but the thing itself a value beyond all inestimable treasure.' So much the more it behoveth us to take care lest we, contenting ourselves with the sweetness of the name, lose and forgo the thing, being of greatest value that can come unto this noble realm. The inestimable treasure is the use of it in this house . . . (15)"

Elizabeth's calm Elizabeth's good sense stopped matters coming to a head. In 1601, near the end of her reign, she accepted the Commons' criticisms of her policy with these words: "I do assure you that there is no prince that loveth his subjects better, or whose love can countervail our love. There is no jewel, be it of never so rich a prize, which I prefer before this jewel: I mean your love. For I do more esteem it than any treasure or riches; for that we know how to prize, but love and thanks I count inestimable.

"And though God hath raised me high, yet this I count the glory of my crown, that I have reigned with your loves. This makes me that I do not so much rejoice that God hath made me to be a queen, as to be a queen over so thankful a people. Therefore I have cause to wish nothing more than to content the subject, and that is a duty which I owe. Neither do I desire to live longer days than that I may see your prosperity, and that's my only desire (16)."

Trouble ahead Yet royal authority remained intact. A book published in

1565 explained: "To be short, the prince is the life, the head and the authority of all things that be done in the realm of England. And to no prince is done more honour and reverence than to the king and queen of England; no man speaketh to the prince nor serveth at the table but in adoration and kneeling; all persons of the realm be bareheaded before him; insomuch that in the chamber of presence, where the cloth of estate is set, no man dare walk, yea though the prince be not there, no man dare tarry there but bareheaded. This is understood of the subjects of the realm: for all strangers be suffered there and in all places to use the manner of their country, such is the civility of our nation (17)."

There lay the danger of trouble in the future: what would happen if Elizabeth should be succeeded by a less diplomatic ruler?

This was just what happened when James Stuart came to the throne in 1603 as James I. In his speeches he asserted the doctrine of divine right—the belief that kings answered to God alone, and had to be obeyed without question by their subjects: "Monarchy is the supremest thing upon earth: for kings are not only God's lieutenants upon earth and sit upon God's throne, but even by God himself they are called gods [and in] the Scriptures kings are called gods, and so their power after a certain relation compared to the Divine power. Kings are also compared to fathers of families: for a king is truly *parens patriae*, the politic father of his people. And lastly, kings are compared to the head of this microcosm of the body of man.

James I and divine right

"To dispute what God may do is blasphemy . . . So it is sedition in subjects to dispute what a king may do in the height of his power. But just kings will ever be willing to declare what they will do, if they will not incur the curse of God. I will not be content that my power be disputed upon, but I shall ever be willing to make the reason appear of all my doings, and rule by actions according to my laws (18)."

A speech which James made to Parliament in 1610 shows how much he repeated these ideas: "Kings are justly called gods for that they exercise a manner or resemblance of Divine power upon earth. For, if you will consider the attributes to God, you shall see how they agree in the person of a king. God hath power

23

CAROLVS DEI GRATIA MAGNÆ BRITANIÆ FRANCIÆ ET HIBERNIÆ REX.

24

to create or destroy, make or unmake, at his pleasure; to give life or send death; to judge all, and to be judged nor accomptable to none; to raise low things and to make high things low at his pleasure; and to God are both soul and body due.

"And the like power have kings: they make and unmake their subjects; they have power of raising and casting down; of life and of death; judges over all their subjects and in all causes, and yet accomptable to none but God only (19)."

What did James intend this to mean in practice? In a speech to the judges of the Star Chamber Court in 1616, he said, "If there fall out a question that concerns my prerogative or mystery of State, deal not with it . . . for they are transcendant matters . . . That which concerns the mystery of the King's power is not lawful to be disputed (20)."

Royal power

After James had made one of these flamboyant speeches, an observer wrote: "I hear it bred generally much discomfort, to see our monarchical power and regal prerogative strained so high, and made so transcendant every way . . . If the practice should follow the positions, we are not likely to leave to our successors that freedom we received from our forefathers (21)."

General alarm

The result was that Parliament, very early in James's reign in 1604, issued an "Apology of the Commons". Here it insisted on its own rights and powers: "The right of the liberty of the Commons of England in Parliament consisteth chiefly in these three things: first, that the shires, cities, and boroughs of England . . . have free choice of such persons as they shall put in trust to represent them.

Parliament protests

"Secondly, that the persons chosen during the time of the Parliament, as also of their access and recess, be free from restraint, arrest, and imprisonment.

"Thirdly, that in Parliament they may speak freely their consciences without check or controlment, doing the same with due reverence to the sovereign court of Parliament—that is, to your majesty and to both the Houses, who all in this case make but one politic body, whereof your highness is the head . . . (22)"

James was soon plunged in the religious issue. When he came to the throne, the Puritans presented him with the Millenary Petition, so-called because it was said to have a thousand

The Millenary Petition

Opposite A contemporary engraving of Charles I

signatures. It asked him to agree to various changes in the Church services:

"That the cross in baptism, interrogatories ministered to infants, confirmation, as superfluous, may be taken away.

"Baptism not to be ministered by women, and so explained;

"The cap and surplice not urged;

"That examination may go before the communion; that it be ministered with a sermon;

"That divers terms of priests and absolution, and some other used, with the ring in marriage, and other such like in the Book, may be corrected;

"The longsomeness of service abridged;

"Church songs and music moderated to better edification;

"That the Lord's Day be not profaned, the rest upon holy days not so strictly urged;

"That there may be an uniformity of doctrine prescribed;

"No Popish opinion to be any more taught or defended;

"No ministers charged to teach their people to bow at the name of Jesus;

"That the canonical Scriptures only be read in the church (23)."

Call for better clergy The petition also asked that the clergy should be better preachers and not neglect their parishes:

"That none hereafter be admitted into the ministry but able and sufficient men, and those to preach diligently, and especially upon the Lord's Day;

"That such as be already entered and cannot preach, may either be removed and some charitable course taken with them for their relief or else to be forced, according to the value of their livings, to maintain preachers;

"That non-residency be not permitted (24)."

James I and the Puritans While King of Scotland before 1603 James had come to dislike Presbyterianism. In his speech at the opening of the English Parliament in 1604 he showed his hostility to the English Puritans: "At my first coming, although I found but one religion, and that which by myself is professed, publicly allowed and by the law maintained, yet found I another sort of religion, besides a private sect, lurking within the bowels of this nation. The first is the true religion [and] the second is the falsely called Catholics, but truly

Papists: the third, which I call a sect rather than a religion, is the Puritans and Novelists, who do not so far differ from us in points of religion [but are] discontented with the present government and impatient to suffer any superiority, which maketh their sect unable to be suffered in any well-governed commonwealth (25)."

James would do no more than hold a conference between some Puritan clergymen and the bishops at Hampton Court Palace. He presided over it himself, but attacked the Puritans all the time, especially when they suggested that laymen should share authority with the bishops. James thought this would be the beginning of Presbyterianism: "The King was somewhat stirred, yet, which is admirable in him, without passion or show thereof; thinking that they aimed at a Scottish presbytery, which, saith he, as well agreed with a monarchy as God and the Devil. Then Jack and Tom and Will and Dick shall meet, and at their pleasures censure me and my Council and all our proceedings. Then Will shall stand up and say, 'It must be thus'; then Dick shall reply and say, 'Nay, marry, but we shall have it thus.' (26)"

Hampton Court Conference

In these words, James showed that he feared that, if the authority of the bishops was undermined in the Church, then the authority of the crown would suffer in the state. He threatened the Puritans in no uncertain terms: "If this be all your party hath to say, I will make them conform themselves, or else I will harry them out of the land, or else do worse (27)."

Royal threats

James's attitude alarmed Parliament. The Commons wanted to make sure that nothing was done about religion without their approval. The Apology of the Commons of 1604 stated: "For matter of religion, it will appear by examination of truth and right that your majesty should be misinformed, if any man should deliver that the kings of England have any absolute power in themselves, either to alter religion (which God forfend should be in the power of any mortal man whatsoever!) or to make any laws concerning the same, otherwise than in temporal causes by consent of Parliament (28)."

Apology of the Commons

James did not heed the warning. The persecution of Puritans continued, and in 1611 the Court of High Commission, created by Elizabeth to enforce the royal supremacy in the Church, was

Puritans persecuted

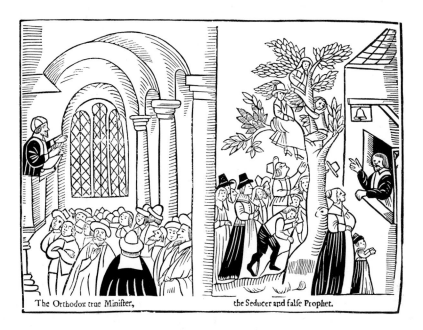

The Orthodox true Minister,   the Seducer and false Prophet.

Above A contemporary woodcut showing the Church of England as the
"true minister", and the more popular, Puritan preacher as the "false
prophet"

Opposite Puritans explaining their views to James I, who disliked and
distrusted them

given more power to stop Puritans expressing their deeply-felt
views: "And also we [do give] authority unto you . . . to inquire
and search for . . . all heretical, schismatical and seditious books,
libels and writings, and all makers, devisers, printers and wilful
dispersers of any such [books] and their procurers, counsellors
and abettors, and the same books [and] the printing presses
themselves likewise to seize, and also to take, apprehend and
imprison . . . the offenders in that behalf (29)."

29

A Puritan woodcut *c.* 1640. It shows the bishops as ungodly men, in comparison with the Puritan clergy

In the face of this persecution some Puritans, as one recorded in his diary, "seeing themselves thus molested, and that there was no hope of their continuance there, by a joint consent they resolved to go into the Low Countries, where they heard was freedom of religion for all men (30)."

These Puritans, who went to Holland, later went to America as the Pilgrim Fathers and in future years were joined by others; but many stayed on in England determined to fight all oppression.

Pilgrim Fathers

Indeed, despite the king's opposition, the Puritans continued to grow in number. Their earnest moral piety impressed many people. Richard Baxter, who later became a Puritan minister, told how his father used to read the Bible aloud to his family on Sundays while the other villagers played riotous games: "Many times my mind was inclined to be among them, and sometimes I broke loose from conscience and joined with them; and the more I did it the more I was inclined to it. But when I heard them call my father Puritan, it did much to cure me and alienate me from them. For I considered that my father's exercise of reading the Scripture was better than theirs, and would surely be better thought on by all men at the last; and I considered what it was for that he and others were thus derided (31)."

Puritan piety

Puritan clergymen were the best preachers, and their influence in those days, when few could read, was enormous. As Dr. Thomas Fuller, the seventeenth-century historian, said: "What won them most repute was their ministers' painful preaching in populous places; it being observed in England that those who hold the helm of the pulpit always steer people's hearts as they please (32)."

Puritan preaching

To add to the arguments in politics and religion, finance also became a subject of dispute. James was short of money, but Parliament so mistrusted him that it would not grant him more. Instead, James tried other ways of raising funds, such as "impositions", or increasing customs duties. This angered Parliament even more. A speaker in the great debate on impositions in the House of Commons in 1610 condemned the King's whole financial policy: "The King is bound to protect merchants from spoil by the enemy . . . It is reason therefore that his expense be

Money troubles

Overleaf The Pilgrim Fathers departing from Holland for the New World and freedom to practise their religion

Queen Henrietta Maria, the wife of Charles I

defrayed out of the profit made by merchants . . . The consequence of this argument is thus far true. The law expects that the King should protect merchants: therefore it alloweth him out of merchandize a revenue for the maintenance of his charge, which is the old custom due, as at first I said, by the common law. But it is no good consequence that therefore he may take what he list [pleases], no more than he may at his pleasure increase that old revenue . . . (33)"

Such was the situation when Charles I succeeded his father on the throne in 1625; and Charles, as Bishop Burnet wrote, was not the best man to deal with its problems: "He loved high and rough methods, but had neither skill to conduct them, nor height of genius to manage them. He hated all who offered prudent and moderate counsels, as proceeding either from republican principles, or a care to preserve themselves by sacrificing his authority. And even when he saw it necessary to follow such advices, yet he still hated those who gave them (34)." *Charles I*

In addition, Charles was much influenced by his Catholic French wife, Henrietta Maria. Her effect upon him, Burnet believed, was thoroughly harmful. The Queen "was a woman of great vivacity in conversation, and loved, all her life long, to be in intrigues of all sorts, but was not so secret in them as such times and such affairs required. She was a woman of no manner of judgment. She was bad at contrivance, but much worse in the execution, but by the liveliness of her discourse she made always a great impression upon the King; and to her little practices, as well as to the King's own temper, the sequel of all his misfortunes was owing (35)." *Queen Henrietta Maria*

Charles's relations with his Parliaments went from bad to worse. If they would not do as he wished, he dissolved them, and even the Earl of Clarendon, staunch Royalist as he was, had to admit the fatal consequences: "Parliaments were summoned, and again dissolved . . . That in the fourth year (after the dissolution of the two former) was determined . . . that there should be no more assemblies of that nature expected, and all men inhibited upon the penalty of censure, so much as to speak of a Parliament . . . No man can shew me a source, from whence these waters of bitterness we now taste have more probably *Relations with Parliament* flowed, than from these unseasonable, unskilful, and precipitate dissolutions of Parliaments (36)."

In religion, Charles supported the Arminian movement in the Church. This movement was led by William Laud, Archbishop of Canterbury; it upheld many of the old practices in the Church that were disliked by the Puritans. Under Arminian influence, it was ordered: "Because experience hath shewed us how irreverent the behaviour of many people is in many places, some leaning, others casting their hats, and some sitting upon, some standing [on], and others sitting under the Communion Table in time of Divine Service, for the avoiding of these and the like abuses it is thought meet and convenient by this present synod that the said Communion Tables in all chancels or chapels be decently severed with rails, to preserve them from such or worse profanations . . . (37)"

To the Puritans, this was to treat the communion table like a medieval altar. They felt sure that Laud was secretly Roman Catholic.

To add to his unpopularity, Laud wished the Church to regain its influence in public life and punish people for moral offences. Clarendon spoke of the resentment Laud aroused by using the Court of High Commission for this purpose: "Persons of honour and great quality were every day cited into the High Commission Court, upon the fame of their incontinence or other scandal in their lives (38)."

Charles linked the crown with this unpopularity by ordering Puritan criticisms to cease. In 1629 he threatened to take action if they did not: "But if we shall be deceived in this our expectation, and that by reading, preaching and making books either *pro* or *contra* concerning these differences men begin anew to dispute, we shall take such order with them and those books, that they shall wish they had never thought upon these needless controversies (39)."

The inevitable result was to worsen the King's relations with Parliament. As Sir John Eliot, a Puritan Member of Parliament, said: "It is observable in the House of Commons as their whole history gives it, that wherever the motion does break forth of the fears or dangers in religion, and the increase of Popery, their

Charles I opening Parliament (1625)

Cancellarij Sedes in

affections are much stirred; and whatever is obnoxious in the State, it then is reckoned as an incident in that (40)."

Moreover, Charles too was short of money. In 1629 he summoned a Parliament to ask it for a grant, only to face deep resentment. The Commons were angry at him for supporting Arminianism, and for levying tunnage (a tax on imported wine) and poundage (a tax on imported and exported goods) without their consent. While the Speaker was held forcibly down in his chair, the Commons passed the famous Three Resolutions:

"1. Whosoever shall bring in innovation of religion, or by favour or countenance seek to extend or introduce Popery or Arminianism, or other opinion disagreeing from the true and orthodox Church, shall be reputed a capital enemy to this Kingdom and Commonwealth.

"2. Whosoever shall counsel or advise the taking and levying of the subsidies of tunnage and poundage, not being granted by Parliament . . . shall be likewise reputed an innovator in the Government, and a capital enemy to the Kingdom and Commonwealth.

"3. If any merchant or person whatsoever shall voluntarily yield, or pay the said subsidies of tunnage and poundage, not being granted by Parliament, he shall likewise be reputed a betrayer of the liberties of England, and an enemy to the same (41)."

The King's answer was to dissolve this Parliament and rule for the next eleven years without one.

During this period of Charles's "personal rule" the religious issue intensified. Hundreds more Puritans emigrated to America as the *Mayflower* pilgrims had done in 1620. As Laud said, the main point was whether bishops were necessary in the Church as part of God's will: "Our main crime is . . . that we are bishops . . . And a great trouble 'tis to them [puritans] that we maintain that our calling of bishops is *jure divino* (42)"—by divine law.

To raise money during these difficult years, Charles used various means such as extending the obligation to pay ship money (for the upkeep of the navy) from coastal to inland towns, a demand which was resisted by John Hampden in 1637.

A contemporary diarist expressed the fears such measures aroused: "By the same right the King, upon like pretence, might gather the same sum ten, twelve or a hundred times redoubled, and so to infinite proportions to any one shire, when and as often as he pleased; and so no man was, in conclusion, worth anything (43)."

How long would Charles be able to rule his kingdom in this way?

2 The First Civil War

AFTER the dramatic events which followed, many looked back on the eleven years of Charles's personal rule as a peaceful and pleasant period. Clarendon wrote eloquently of how it ended: "In this blessed conjuncture, when no other prince thought he wanted any thing to compass what he most desired to be possessed of, but the affection and friendship of the king of England, a small, scarce discernible cloud arose in the north, which was shortly after attended with such a storm, that never gave over raging till it had shaken, and even rooted up, the greatest and tallest cedars of the three nations; blasted all its beauty and fruitfulness; brought its strength to decay, and its glory to reproach, and almost to desolation; by such a career and deluge of wickedness and rebellion, as by not being enough foreseen, or in truth suspected, could not be prevented (44)."

The "cloud in the north" came from Scotland. In 1637 a new Prayer Book of an anti-Puritan character was introduced into the Church of Scotland, but it provoked rioting. Edward Phillips, John Milton's nephew, described what is said to have happened in St. Giles' Cathedral, Edinburgh: "No sooner was the Book opened by the Dean of Edinburgh, but a number of the meaner sort, with clapping of their hands and outcries, made a great uproar; and one of them, called Jane or Janot Gaddis (yet living at the writing of this relation), flung a little folding-stool, whereon she sat, at the Dean's head, saying, 'Out thou false thief! dost thou say the mass at my lug?' Which was followed with so great a noise (45)."

Charles tried to crush the rebellious Scots in 1639, but they were too strong for his weak forces. He summoned the Short Parliament of 1640, but it refused to pay for an army to fight the Scots. He dissolved it and was defeated by the Scots. Clarendon described his plight: "The Scots, upon this defeat,

41

Opposite The riots in St. Giles's Cathedral, Edinburgh, which followed the introduction of the new anti-Puritan Prayer Book

became masters of a great part of the north, and the King's affairs were reduced to great perplexity. His treasure was gone, his subjects were irritated, and his ministry all frightened, as exposed to the anger and justice of the Parliament; so that he had brought himself into great straits, but had not the dexterity to extricate himself out of them (46)."

Oliver Cromwell

Charles was compelled to summon another Parliament in 1640, the Long Parliament. A member of both the Short and Long Parliaments was a Huntingdonshire squire called Oliver Cromwell. He was inconspicuous then, but was destined to bring Charles to execution and replace him as ruler of the country. A young courtier, Sir Philip Warwick, recalled seeing Cromwell for the first time: "I came one morning into the House well clad, and perceived a gentleman speaking (whom I knew not) very ordinarily apparelled; for it was a plain cloth-suit which seemed to have been made by an ill country tailor. His linen was plain, and not very clean, and I remember a speck or two of blood upon his little band, which was not much larger than his collar; his hat was without a hat-band. His stature was of good size, his sword stuck close to his side, his countenance swollen and reddish, his voice sharp and untunable, and his eloquence full of fervour; for the subject matter would not bear much of reason . . . (47)"

Cromwell's religion

Cromwell was a convinced Independent, resolved to throw himself into the cause of his religion. He wrote fervently in a letter in 1638: "My soul is with the congregation of the first-born, my body rests in hope, and if here I may honour God either by doing or by suffering, I shall be most glad (48)."

Supporters on trial

The Long Parliament was determined to take advantage of the King's plight. It struck at his supporters. Archbishop Laud was thrown into the Tower and later executed. Immediate charges were brought against Thomas Wentworth, Earl of Strafford, who had been regarded as the strong man behind the throne. At his trial, he stated: "I did ever inculcate this—that the happiness of a kingdom consists of a just poise of the King's prerogative and the subject's liberty; and that things would never go well till they went hand in hand together (49)."

Both Royalists and Parliamentarians agreed with this, but

Above Thomas Wentworth, Earl of Strafford, whose execution Charles I was unable to prevent, an injustice which troubled him until his own execution

Below The scene outside the Tower of London when Strafford was executed in 1641

A. Doctor Vsher Lord
te of Ireland,
B the Sherifes of London
C the Earle of Straffor
D his kindred and Frie

neither could trust the other. Strafford was sentenced to death, but Charles sent him a letter: "The misfortune that is fallen upon you [is] such that I must lay by the thought of employing you hereafter in my affairs. Yet I cannot satisfy myself in honour or conscience without assuring you (now in the midst of your troubles), that upon the word of a king you shall not suffer in life, honour, or fortune. This is but justice, and therefore a very mean reward from a master to so faithful and able a servant as you have showed yourself to be; yet it is as much as I conceive the present times will permit (50)."

But Charles did not dare to pardon Strafford, and his faithful minister was executed in 1641. A few years later, as he himself mounted the scaffold, Charles revealed how much it lay on his conscience.

In 1641 the Commons accepted the so-called Root and Branch Petition signed by some 15,000 Londoners. It protested against the Laudian practices introduced into the Church: "The great conformity and likeness both continued and increased of our Church to the Church of Rome, in vestures, postures, ceremonies and administrations, namely as bishops' rotchets and the lawn-sleeves, the four-cornered cap, the cope and surplice, the tippet, the hood and the canonical coat, the pulpits clothed, especially now of late, with the Jesuits' badge upon them every way.

"The standing up at *Gloria Patri*, and at the reading of the Gospel, praying towards the east, bowing at the name of Jesus, the bowing to the altar towards the east, cross in baptism, the kneeling at the Communion (51)."

Most members would have agreed with this, but many would not accept another clause in the Petition: "Moreover, the offices and jurisdictions of archbishops, lordbishops, deans, arch-deacons, being the same way of Church government which is in the Romish Church, and which was in England in the time of Popery, little change thereof being made (except only the head from whence it was derived), the same arguments supporting the Pope which do uphold the prelates, and overthrowing the prelates which do pull down the Pope; and other Reformed Churches having, upon their rejection of the Pope, cast the prelates out also, as members of the Beast (52)." Such a "root and branch" attack on the Church produced the first signs of division in Parliament.

King Charles paid a brief visit to Scotland in a vain effort to get help there. He wrote a letter to the Clerk of the Council seeking to rally Churchmen to his side: "I hear it is reported that I am resolved, at my return, to alter the form of the Church government in England to this here. Therefore I command you to assure all my servants there, that I am constant for the doctrine and discipline of the Church of England, as it was established by Queen Elizabeth and my father; and resolve by the grace of God to live and die in the maintenance of it (53)."

King and Commons

Alarmed by the growing strength of the Church's supporters, the Commons drew up a "Grand Remonstrance" which set out their grievances and demanded religious reforms. It was passed only by eleven votes. "Had it been rejected," Cromwell said, "I would have sold all I had the next morning and never have seen England any more, and I know there are many other honest men

Charles arriving at the House of Commons in his attempt to arrest five dissident members

Uniforms worn by militiamen during the reign of Charles I

of this same resolution." Clarendon observed, "So near was the poor kingdom at that time to its deliverance."

The Five Members   Early in 1642 Charles was urged by Queen Henrietta Maria to seize five of the leading members of the opposition in the House of Commons who were mainly responsible for the Remonstrance. But as Richard Baxter described, it was a disastrous fiasco: "Another great cause of the diffidence and war was this: the King . . . goeth to the House of Commons with a company of cavaliers with swords and pistols, to have charged five of the members of that House, and one of the Lords' House, with high treason. But the King was not so secret or speedy in this action but the members had notice of it before his coming, and absented themselves . . . and so the King and his company laid hands on none, but went their ways. Had the five members been there, the rest supposed they would have taken them away by violence (54)."

Hostility towards Charles   Charles was the first to use violence, and Clarendon noted the hostile reception Charles received the next day from the people of London: "In his passage through the city, the rude people flocking together and crying out, 'Privilege of Parliament, privilege of Parliament'; some of them passing very near his own

46

A Roundhead cavalryman (*left*) and a pikeman (*right*) at the time of the Civil Wars

coach, and amongst the rest one calling out with a very loud voice, 'To your tents, O Israel' (55)."

Meanwhile in the autumn of 1641, a rebellion had broken out in Ireland, where Protestant settlers were massacred. Baxter described the alarm it caused in England: "This filled all England with a fear both of the Irish and of the Papists at home, for they supposed that the priests and the interest of their religion were the cause. Insomuch, that when the rumour of a plot was occasioned at London, the poor people, all the countries [counties] over, were ready either to run to arms or hide themselves, thinking that the Papists were ready to rise and cut their throats (56)." *Irish Rebellion*

Charles announced that he would take personal command of an army to put down the Irish revolt. But Parliament would not trust him with troops, and refused to agree. Charles wrote to both Houses of Parliament in April 1642: "We are so troubled and astonished to find the unexpected reception and misunderstanding of our message of the eighth of April, concerning our Irish journey, that, being so much disappointed of the approbation and thanks we looked for to that declaration, we have great *Parliament refuses troops*

47

cause to doubt whether it be in our power to say or do anything which shall not fall within the like interpretation.

"But, as we have in that message called God to witness the sincerity of the profession of our only ends for the undertaking that journey, so we must appeal to all our good subjects, and the whole world, whether the reasons alleged against that journey be of weight to satisfy our understanding, or the counsel presented to dissuade us from it be full of that duty as is like to prevail over our affections (57)."

Parliament raises an army

The Irish revolt brought civil war in England much closer, for when Parliament proceeded to raise a militia of its own, Lord Paget was among many others who was shocked into supporting the King: "When I found a preparation of arms against the King under a shadow of loyalty, I rather resolved to obey a good conscience than particular ends, and am now on my way to His Majesty, where I will throw myself down at his feet and die a loyal subject (58)."

Reluctant loyalty

Others, as the country drifted into war, felt bound to declare themselves Royalists, but did so reluctantly. One of these was Sir Edmund Verney: "I do not like the quarrel, and do heartily wish that the King would yield and consent to what they [Parliament] desire; so that my conscience is only concerned in honour and in gratitude to follow my master. I have eaten his bread and served him near thirty years, and will not do so base a thing as to forsake him; and choose rather to lose my life, which I am sure to do, to preserve and defend those things which are against my conscience to preserve and defend: for I will deal freely with you, I have no reverence for the bishops, for whom this quarrel [subsists] (59)."

Royalists

Baxter described those who supported the King: "A great part of the Lords forsook the Parliament, and so did many of the House of Commons, and came to the King; but that was, for the most of them, after Edgehill fight, when the King was at Oxford. A very great part of the knights and gentlemen of England in the several counties (who were not Parliament men) adhered to the King . . . And most of the tenants of these gentlemen, and also most of the poorest of the people . . . did follow the gentry and were for the King (60)."

Above The contrast between the fashions worn by Cavaliers and Puritans
Overleaf Cavalier foot and cavalry soldiers

He also told of those who supported Parliament: "On the Parliament's side were besides themselves the smaller part (as some thought) of the gentry in most of the counties, and the greatest part of the tradesmen and freeholders and the middle sort of men, especially in those corporations and counties which depend on clothing and such manufactures . . . (61)"

Religion not politics In Baxter's view, people were moved to support one side or the other by religion rather than politics: "But though it must be confessed that the public safety and liberty wrought very much with most, especially with the nobility and gentry who adhered to the Parliament, yet it was principally the differences about religious matter that filled up the Parliament's armies and put the resolution and valour into their soldiers, which carried them on in another manner than mercenary soldiers . . . (62)."

The better men Later, he believed, still more people were attracted to the Parliamentary side by its religion: "And abundance of the ignorant sort of the country, who were civil, did flock in to the Parliament, and filled up their armies afterward, merely because they heard men *swear* for the Common Prayer and bishops, and heard others *pray* that were against them; and because they heard the King's soldiers with horrid oaths abuse the name of God, and saw them live in debauchery, and the Parliament's soldiers flock to sermons and talking of religion, and praying and singing Psalms together on their guards. And all the sober men that I was acquainted with, who were against the Parliament, were wont to say, 'The King hath the better cause, but the Parliament hath the better men' . . . (63)"

Social unrest Other support was given to the Parliamentary side through a combination of popular religious and social urges, which found expression in a rhyme of the time (64):

> *Since then the anti-Christian crew*
> *Be pressed and over-thrown,*
> *We'll teach the nobles how to crouch,*
> *And keep the gentry down;*
> *Good manners hath an ill report,*
> *And turns to pride we see;*
> *We'll therefore cry all manners down,*
> *And hey then up go we.*

The start of the Civil War, Charles I raising his standard at Nottingham,
August 25th, 1642

There were those, however, who chose for political reasons. *Defence of* One was Colonel Hutchinson. His wife wrote, "He applied *liberty* himself to understand the things then in dispute, and read all the public papers that came forth between the King and Parliament ... Hereby he became abundantly informed in his understanding, and convinced in conscience of the righteousness of the Parliament's cause in point of civil right; and though he was satisfied of the endeavours to introduce popery and subvert the true Protestant religion, which indeed was apparent to every one that impartially considered it, yet he did not think that so clear a ground for the war as the defence of the just English liberties (65)."

Cromwell seems to have shared this point of view when he *Cromwell's* said: "Religion was not the thing at first contested for, but God *view* brought it to that issue at last and gave it unto us by way of redundancy, and at last it proved that which was most dear to us (66)."

War came in the summer of 1642 when Charles raised his *Declaration of* standard in Nottingham Castle. Clarendon recalled little *War* 53 enthusiasm for hostilities: "According to the proclamation, upon the twenty-fifth day of August, the standard was erected, about six of the clock on the evening of a very stormy and tempestuous day. The King himself, with a small train, rode to the top of the castle-hill, Varney the knight-marshal, who was standard-bearer, carrying the standard, which was then erected in the place, with little other ceremony than the sound of drums and trumpets (67)."

Royal clemency   Unlike most civil wars, the English Civil War was fought with restraint on both sides. It was marked by none of the atrocities that were perpetrated in the Thirty Years' War (1618–48) which was then being fought in Germany. This letter was written by Charles to the Mayor of Newbury on the day after the Battle of Newbury in September, 1643: "Our will and command is, that you forthwith send into the towns and villages adjacent, and bring thence all the sick and hurt soldiers of the Earl of Essex's army; and though they be rebels, and deserve the punishment of traitors, yet out of our tender compassion upon them as being our subjects, our will and pleasure is, that you carefully provide for their recovery, as well as for those of our own army, and then to send them to Oxford (68)."

Parliament seeks compromise   At first the Parliamentary leaders were Presbyterians. They wanted to end the war by compromise rather than victory. One of them, the Earl of Manchester, said in 1642 "that war would never be ended by the sword but by accommodation, and that he would not have it ended by the sword, and that if we should beat the King ninety-nine times, and he beat us but once, we should all be hanged (69)."

Cromwell determined   Cromwell, however, was determined to beat the enemy. He said, "If the King chanced to be in the body of the enemy that he was to charge, he would as soon discharge his pistol upon him as at any other private person (70)."

New Model Army   He set about raising a force, which became known as the New Model Army. It was composed of men who shared his political outlook and religion. He told his recruiters at Cambridge in the winter of 1642–43: "God hath given it to our handful: let us endeavour to keep it. I had rather have a plain russet-coated captain that knows what he fights for, and loves what he knows, than that which you call 'a gentleman' and is nothing else (71)."

The formation of the New Model Army was a turning point in the war, as was Scottish intervention. Under the Solemn League and Covenant the Scots agreed to provide an army to fight in the common cause against the King: "We shall also, according to our places and callings, in this common cause of religion, liberty and peace of the kingdom, assist and defend all those that enter into this league and covenant, in the maintaining and pursuing thereof; and shall not suffer ourselves . . . to be divided and withdrawn from this blessed union and conjunction. [We shall not] make defection to the contrary part, or give ourselves to a detestable indifferency or neutrality in this cause, which so much concerneth the glory of God, the good of the kingdoms, and the honour of the King (72)."

The Covenant was a religious agreement, too, which looked forward to the time when Presbyterianism would be established in England: "And this covenant we make in the presence of Almighty God, the Searcher of all hearts, with a true intention to perform the same, as we shall answer at that great day when the secrets of all hearts shall be disclosed; most humbly beseeching the Lord to strengthen us by His Holy Spirit for this end, and to bless our desires and proceedings with such success as may be a deliverance and safety to His people, and encouragement to the Christian Churches (73)."

At the same time, disunity was appearing in the Royalist ranks. Charles wrote to the Earl of Newcastle in the spring of 1644: "By your last dispatch I perceive that the Scots are not the only, or (it may be said) the enemies you contest withal, at this time; wherefore I must tell you a word (for I have not time to make long discourses), you must as much condemn the impertinent or malicious tongues and pens of those that are, or profess to be your friends, as well as you despise the sword of an equal enemy (74)."

Throughout 1644 the faith and efficiency of the New Model Army carried it to victory. After the Royalists under Prince Rupert were routed at the Battle of Marston Moor in July, Cromwell wrote: "Truly England and the Church of God hath had a great favour from the Lord, in this great victory given unto

Overleaf An engagement during the battle of Marston Moor, in which the New Model Army routed the Royalists

us, such as the like never was since this war began. It had all the evidences of an absolute victory obtained by the Lord's blessing upon the Godly Party principally.

"We never charged but we routed the enemy. The left wing, which I commanded, being our own horse saving a few Scots in our rear, beat all the Prince's horse. God made them as stubble to our swords. We charged their regiments of foot with our horse, and routed all we charged. The particulars I cannot relate now, but I believe of twenty-thousand the Prince hath not four-thousand left. Give glory, all the glory, to God (75)."

The Parliamentarian victory at Naseby the next summer virtually ended the war. From France, Queen Henrietta Maria advised Charles to abandon the Church of England if necessary to reach an agreement with the victors. Charles replied, "Albeit that my personal danger must of necessity precede thine, yet thy safety seems to be hazarded by my resolution concerning Church government. I am doubly grieved to differ with thee in opinion, though I am confident that my judgement, not love, is censured by thee for it. But I hope, whatsoever thou mayst wish, thou wilt not blame me at all, if thou rightly understand the state of the question. For I assure thee, I put little or no difference between setting up the Presbyterian government, or submitting to the Church of Rome. Therefore make the case thine own. With what patience wouldst thou give ear to him who should persuade thee, for worldly respects, to leave the communion of the Roman Church for any other? Indeed, sweetheart, this is my case; for, suppose my concession in this should prove but temporary, it may palliate though not excuse my sin (76)."

Charles and the Church

Charles showed the same attachment to the Church in a letter written at the same time to his son, the Prince of Wales (later Charles II): "I command you, upon my blessing, to be constant to your religion, neither hearkening to Roman superstitions, nor the seditious and schismatical doctrines of the Presbyterians and Independents. For I know that a persecuted Church is not thereby less pure, though less fortunate (77)."

Royal constancy

Opposite Charles at the battle of Naseby, when his troops were defeated again

A Solemn
LEAGUE AND COVENANT,
for Reformation, and defence of
Religion, the Honour and happinesse
of the king, and the Peace and safety of the
three kingdomes of
ENGLAND, SCOTLAND, and IRELAND.

We Noblemen, Barons, Knights, Gentlemen, Citizens, Burgesses, Ministers of the Gospel, and Commons of all sorts in the Kingdomes of England, Scotland, and Ireland, by the Providence of God, living under one king and being of one reformed Religion, having before our eyes the Glory of God, and the advancement of the kingdome of our Lord and Saviour Jesus Christ, the Honour and happinesse of the kings Majesty and his posterity, and the true publique Liberty, Safety, and Peace of the kingdomes wherein every ones private Condition is included, and calling to minde the treacherous and Bloody Plots, Conspiracies, Attempts, and Practices of the Enemies of God, against the true Religion, and professors thereof in all places, especially in these three Kingdomes ever since the Reformation of Religion, and how much their rage, power and presumption, are of late, and at this time increased and exercised, whereof the deplorable state of the Church and kingdom of Ireland, the distressed estate of the Church and Kingdom of England, and the dangerous state of the Church and kingdom of Scotland, are present and publique Testimonies; We have now at last, after other means of Supplication, Remonstrance, Protestations, and Sufferings, for the preservation of our selves and our Religion, from utter Ruine and Destruction, according to the commendable practice of these Kingdoms in former times, and the Example of Gods people in other Nations, after mature deliberation, resolved and determined to enter into a mutuall and solemn League and Covenant, wherein we all subscribe, and each one of us for himself, with our hands lifted up to the most high God, do sweare.

A Malignant   A Priest

I That we shall sincerely, really and constantly, through the Grace of God, endeavour in our severall places and callings, the preservation of the Reformed Religion in the Church of Scotland, in Doctrine, Worship, Discipline & Government, against our common Enemies, the reformation of Religion in the kingdomes of England and Ireland in Doctrine, Worship, Discipline and Government, according to the Word of God, and the Example of the best Reformed Churches. And shall indeavour to bring the Churches of God in the three kingdoms, to the neerest conjunction and Uniformity in Religion, Confession of Faith, Form of Church government, Directory for Worship and Catechising, That we and our posterity after us may as Brethren live in Faith and Love, and the Lord may delight to dwell in the midest of us.

Thou hast avouched ye Lord this day to be thy God, and to walk in his wayes & to keep his Statutes & his Commandments & his Judgements & to hearken to his voyce. And the Lord hath avouched thee this day to be his peculiar people & to make thee high above all nations in prayse & name & in honour.
Deut: 26: 17 18

II That we shall in like manner without respect of persons indeavour the extirpation of Popery, Prelacie, (that is Church government by Arch-Bishops, Bishops, their Chancellors and Commissaries, Deans, Deans and Chapters, Archdeacons & all other Ecclesiasticall Officers depending on that Hierarchy) Superstition, Heresie, Schisme, Prophanenesse, and what soever shall be found to be contrary to sound Doctrine, and the power of Godlinesse, lest we partake in other mens sins, and therby be in danger to receive of their plagues, and that the Lord may be one and has Name one in the three kingdomes.

Euery plant which my heauenly Father hath not planted shall be rooted out. Mat: 15:

Comforts   Shops

III We shall with the same sincerity, reallity and constancy, in our severall Vocations, endeavour with our estates and lives, mutually to preserve the Rights and Priviledges of the Parliaments, and the Liberties of the kingdomes, and to preserve and defend the kings Majesties person and authority, in the preservation and defence of the true Religion, and Liberties of the kingdomes, that the World may beare witnesse with our consciences of our Loyalltie, and that we have no thoughts or intentions to diminish his Majesties just power and greatnesse.

The Lord will Create upon euery dwelling place & vpon Sion & vpon her Assemblies

A Cloud and smoke by day and a shining of a flaming Fire by night, for vpon all the glory shall be a defence. Isaiah: 4: 5

IV We shall also with all faithfulnesse endeavour the discovery of all such as have beene, or shall be Incendiaries, Malignants, or evill Instruments by hindering the Reformation of Religion, dividing the king from his people, or one of the kingdoms from another, or making any faction or parties amongst the people, contrary to this league & Covenant, that they may be brought to publick triall, and receive condigne punishment, as the degree of their offences shall require or deserve, or the supreme Judicatories of both kingdoms respectively, or others having power from them for that effect, shall judge convenient.

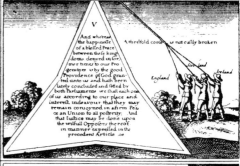

I will grace out vaine imaginations, the Rebells & throw their train free, & assault me

I will bring them forth out of the Countries where they sojourne. Ezemel. 20: 35:38

V
And whereas the happinesse of a blessed Peace between these kingdoms denyed in former times to our Progenitors is by the good Providence of God granted unto us, and hath been lately concluded and setled by both Parliaments we shall each one of us according to our place and interest, indeavour that they may remain conjoyned in a firm Peace or an Union to all posterity. And that Justice may be done upon the wilfull Opposites thereof in manner expressed in the precedent Article.

A threefold cord is not easily broken

Scotland
England   Ireland

VI We shall also according to our places & callings in this common cause of Religion, Liberty and Peace of the kingdomes assist and defend all those that enter into this League and Covenant, in the maintaining & pursuing thereof, and shall not suffer our selves directly or indirectly by whatsoever combination, perswasion or terror to be devided & withdrawn from this blessed Unio & conjunction, whether to make defection to the contrary part, or to give our selves to a detestable indifferency or neutrality in this cause which so much concerneth the glory of God, the good of the kingdomes, and honour of the king; but shall all the dayes of our lives zealously and constantly continue therein, against all opposition, and promote the same according to our power, against all Lets and impediments whatsoever, and what we are not able our selves to suppresse or overcome, we shall reveale and make known, that it may be timely prevented or removed. All which we shall do as in the sight of God.

And his heart shall be ioyned with the holy Covenant Dan: 11:28

And because these kingdoms are guilty of many sins & provocations against God & his Son Iesus Christ, as is too manifest by our present distresses and dangers the fruits thereof. We professe and declare before God and the world our unfaigned desire to be humbled for our sins for the sins of these kingdoms especially that we have not as we ought, valued the inestimable benefit of the Gospel, that we have not laboured for the purity and power thereof, and that we have not endeavored to receive Christ in our hearts, not to walk worthy of him in our lives, which are the causes of other sins and transgressions so much abounding amongst us. And our true and unfaigned purpose desire and endeavour for our selves and all others under our power and charge, both in publick and in private, in all duties we owe to God and man to amend our lives, and each one to go before another in the Example, of a reall Reformation that the Lord may turne away his wrath, and heavy indignation and establish these Churches and kingdoms in truth and peace. And this Covenant we make in the presence of almighty God, the Searcher of all hearts, with a true intention to performe the same, as we shall answer at that great day when the secrets of all hearts shall be disclosed. Most humbly beseeching the Lord to strengthen us by his Holy Spirit for this end, and to blesse our desires & proceedings with such successe, as may be deliverance and safety to his people, & encouragement to other Christian Churches groaning under or in danger of the yoake of Anti-christian Tyranny to joyne in the same, or like Association and Covenant, to the glory of God, the enlargement of the kingdom of Iesus Christ, and the peace and tranquility of Christian kingdoms & Commonwealths.

3 The Captive King

ON A MARCH MORNING in 1646, the King's sole remaining
forces were defeated at Stow-on-the-Wold. Their commander,
Sir Jacob Astley, sitting on a drum said cheerfully to his captors:
"Well, boys, you have done your work and may go home and
play—unless you will fall out with one another (78)." *End of the war*

Charles, indeed, hoped to benefit from disagreements among
his enemies. Early in May, 1646, he rode into the camp of the
Scottish army which was besieging Newark and surrendered to
its commander. The Scots took him northward to Newcastle-
upon-Tyne, but their talks with him failed because he would
have nothing to do with Presbyterianism. Then the English
Parliament sent him the so-called "Propositions of Newcastle",
which required him to take the Solemn League and Covenant
and accept Parliamentary control of the army for twenty years. *Newcastle*
Propositions

Charles showed his attitude towards these proposals in a
letter to some friends: "It is not the change of Church government which is chiefly aimed at (though that were too much),
but it is by that pretext to take away the dependency of the
Church from the crown, which, let me tell you, I hold to be of
equal consequence to that of the militia; for people are governed
by the pulpit more than the sword in times of peace (79)."

A few days later he sent his answer to Parliament: "His
Majesty desires and proposeth to come to London . . . upon the
public faith and security of the two Houses of his Parliament,
and the Scots Commissioners, that he shall be there with freedom, honour and safety; where by his personal presence he
may not only raise a mutual confidence between him and his
people, but also have these doubts cleared, and these difficulties
explained unto him, which he now conceives to be destructive to
his just regal power, if he should give a full consent to these
propositions as they now stand (80)." *The King's reply*

Charles was clearly being evasive. He hoped that if the talks *Playing for time*

Opposite The Solemn League and Covenant, presented by Parliament to
Charles in 1643

went on long enough, he would be allowed to continue the meeting in London. He therefore ended his answer with a vague statement that might give Parliament hope for success: "His Majesty assures them, that as he can never condescend unto what is absolutely destructive to that just power which, by the laws of God and the land, he is born unto; so he will cheerfully grant and give his assent unto all such Bills (at the desires of his two Houses), or reasonable demands for Scotland, which shall be really for the good and peace of his people, not having regard to his own particular (much less of anybody's else) in respect of the happiness of these kingdoms (81)."

The King surrenders   The actual result was that the Scots, realizing that Charles would never take the Covenant, handed him over in February, 1647, to the English Parliament in exchange for their arrears of army pay. He was lodged at Holmby House in Northamptonshire under a Parliamentary Commissioner, Richard Graves, but the army feared the Presbyterian-dominated Parliament.

A troop of horse was sent to seize Charles. It was commanded by Cornet Joyce, who wrote a hurried note to Cromwell: "We have secured the King. Graves is run away, he got out about one o'clock in the morning and so went his way. It is suspected he is gone to London, you may imagine what he will do there. You must hasten an answer to us and let us know what we shall do. We are resolved to obey no orders but the General's; we shall follow the Commissioners' directions while we are here, if just in our eyes. I humbly entreat you to consider what is done and act accordingly with all haste you can. We shall not rest till we hear from you (82)."

A wise surrender   Charles was quite ready to go with the army because his talks with Parliament were nearly over, and he was ready to try his skill with the soldiers. A contemporary wrote: "I believe his Majesty had no reason to be very fond of the place where he was before, or of the great respects he received there, being without doubt at the top of his preferment, and in all likelihood not to have continued so well had not some stronger bridle than that of allegiance to him or religion to God made them forbear any further attempt (83)."

Charles was taken to the military headquarters at Newmarket.

Opposite, above The Peers of the Realm greeting Charles as he arrives to open Parliament. *Below* Charles in the House of Lords

Gratious Soueraigne

There the army gave him its terms, the Heads of the Proposals, which included keeping the Church of England, tolerating all Protestants, and giving Parliament control of the army for ten years. Once again, Charles gave an evasive reply: "His Majesty conceives [the Propositions of Parliament] as being destructive to the main principal interests of the army, and of all those whose affections concur with them; and His Majesty having seen the Proposals of the army . . . believes his two Houses will think with him that they much more conduce to the satisfaction of all interests and may be a fitter foundation for a lasting peace than the Propositions [now tendered by Parliament]. He therefore propounds (as the best way in his judgment in order to peace) that his two Houses would instantly take into consideration those Proposals (84)."

Playing off
enemies

Moreover, he put forward a suggestion which showed that he hoped to play off Parliament and the army against each other—and so recover as much of his power as possible. He suggested "that his two Houses would instantly take into consideration those Proposals, upon which there may be a personal treaty with His Majesty, and upon such other Propositions as His Majesty shall make, hoping that the said Proposals may be so moderated in the said treaty as to render them the more capable of His Majesty's full concessions, wherein he resolves to give full satisfaction unto his people for whatsoever shall concern the settling of the Protestant profession, with liberty to tender consciences, and the securing of the laws, liberties and properties of all his subjects, and the just privileges of Parliament for the future (85)."

Pressure on
Parliament

Finally, the King brought all the pressure he could upon Parliament to make it accept his suggestion: "His Majesty therefore conjures his two Houses of Parliament by the duty they owe to God and His Majesty their King, and by the bowels of compassion they have to their fellow subjects . . . that they will forthwith accept His Majesty's offer, whereby the joyful news of peace may be restored to this distressed kingdom (86)."

Ireton's warning

General Ireton warned the King: "Sir, you have the intention to be an arbitrator between the Parliament and us, and we mean to be it between your Majesty and the Parliament (87)."

Gumberg Library
Duquesne University
Pittsburgh, Pa 15282

01/06/1998

Borrower ID: 60098625058829102
Since you have not returned the overdue item(s) listed, you
are being billed and your borrowing privileges are suspended.

ITEM ID	TITLE	DATE DUE	AGENCY	AMOUNT
3528200127295	The trial and executio	12/15/97	3RD FLR	$ 75.00
3528200178826	A coffin for King Char	12/15/97	3RD FLR	$ 75.00
			TOTAL	$150.00

Renewed 7.1
4/30/98
renewed till 8/5/98 mja

ALBERT C LABRIOLA
249 TARA DRIVE
PITTSBURGH, PA 15236

The Presbyterian leaders in Parliament hesitated between Charles and Cromwell—but they were beginning to fear the Independent-led army most. So they began to turn towards the King. But it was too late: they were ruined by their indecision. Clarendon contrasted their methods with those of the Independents: "The Independents always did that which, how ill and unjustifiable whatsoever, contributed still to the end they aimed at . . . whereas the Presbyterians, for the most part, did always

General Ireton, a commander in the rebel army

somewhat that reasonably must destroy their own end, and cross that which they first and principally designed (88)."

When Parliament seemed ready to reopen talks with the King, the army's reply was to occupy London, establish its headquarters at Putney, and take Charles to Hampton Court. By now many of the soldiers had lost all interest in negotiations. In October, 1647, a meeting of the Army Council (which included delegates from each regiment) met in Putney Parish Church. There a member of Cromwell's regiment of horse, Edward Sexby, spoke: "The cause of our misery is upon two things. We sought to satisfy all men and it was well; but in going about to do it we have dissatisfied all men. We have laboured to please a King, and I think, except we go about to cut all our throats we shall not please him; and we have gone to support an house which will prove rotten studds, I mean the Parliament, which consists of a company of rotten members (89)."

His words to the two commanders, Cromwell and Ireton, were outspoken: "One thing I must say to General Cromwell and General Ireton themselves. Your credit and reputation hath been much blasted upon two accounts—your dealings with the King, your plan of settlement which was to satisfy everybody and has satisfied nobody, and your dealings with Parliament.

"The authority of Parliament is a thing which most here would give their lives for, but the Parliament to which we would loyally subject ourselves has still to be called. In my conscience I think these things are the causes of all the reproach that has been cast on you. Consider what we soldiers have to propose, and if you find it reasonable, join with us. So may the kingdom have peace: so may your fellow-soldiers be quieted in spirit (90)."

Prominent among the soldiers in the debate were the extreme democrats, the Levellers. This group presented to the Council an "Agreement of the People", which called for frequent Parliaments, universal suffrage and low taxation: "These things we declare to be our native rights, and therefore are agreed and resolved to maintain them with our utmost possibilities, against all opposition whatsoever ... Having long expected, and dearly earned the establishment of those certain rules of government [we] are yet made to depend for the settlement of our peace and

John Lilburne, the leader of the religious sect known as the Levellers

freedom upon him that intended our bondage, and brought a cruel war upon us (91)."

Cromwell objected strongly to the Levellers' petition: "Would it not be utter confusion? Would it not make England like the Switzerland country, one canton of the Switz against another and one county against another? It is not enough for us to propose good things, but it behoves honest men and Christians that really will approve themselves so before God and men, to see whether or no they be in a condition to attempt, whether, taking all things into consideration, they may honestly endeavour and attempt that that is fairly and plausibly proposed (92)."

Cromwell's reaction

In the discussion that followed, a colonel urged: "I think that the poorest he that is in England hath a life to live as the greatest he. And therefore truly, Sir, I think it's clear, that every man

A colonel's ideas

67

that is to live under a government ought first by his own consent to put himself under that government; and I do think that the poorest man in England is not at all bound in a strict sense to that government that he hath not had a voice to put himself under (93)."

A general
replies

To this General Ireton retorted: "Give me leave to tell you, that if you make this the rule, I think you must fly for refuge to an absolute natural right, and you must deny all civil right (94)."

The King's
escape

The wild language in the Council alarmed Charles. He escaped to the Isle of Wight, as Cromwell wrote to the Speaker of the House of Commons: "His Majesty was expected at supper, when the Commissioners and Colonel Whalley missed him; upon which they entered the room: they found his Majesty had left his cloak behind him in the gallery in the private way. He passed, by the backstairs and vault, towards the waterside (95)."

Letter from the
King

Charles left behind at Hampton Court a dignified letter explaining his action, and casting doubt upon the sincerity of the army leaders. Had he not "just cause to free myself from the hands of those who change their principles . . . and who are not ashamed openly to intend the destruction of the nobility, by taking away their negative voice—and with whom the Levellers' doctrine is rather countenanced than punished?

"Nor would I have this my retirement misinterpreted: for I shall [press for] a safe and well-grounded peace, wherever I am or shall be, and that . . . without the effusion of more Christian blood: for which how many times have I desired, pressed to be heard, and yet no ear given to me?

"And can any reasonable man think, that according to the ordinary course of affairs there can be a settled peace without it, or that God will bless those who refuse to hear their own King? Surely, no (96)."

Dealing with
the Scots

Charles had hoped to be free on the Isle of Wight. Instead, he was held prisoner in Carisbrooke Castle by the island's governor, Colonel Robert Hammond. Charles was able, however, to hold talks with the Scots, rumours of which reached the army. There is a story that one night, late in November, Cromwell and Ireton disguised themselves as troopers and waited at the Blue Boar Inn, Holborn, for an emissary, who bore unwittingly, sewed

Above A print of 1648, showing Charles imprisoned in Carisbrooke Castle. He remained there from November 1647 until December 1648

in his horse's saddle, an important letter from the King to the Queen. When the messenger arrived, his saddle was ripped open, to reveal the letter, "in which the King had acquainted the Queen that he was now courted by both the factions, the Scotch Presbyterians and the Army, and which bid fairest for him should have him, but he thought he should close with the Scots sooner than the other (97)."

On Boxing Day 1647, Charles made an agreement—the "Engagement"—with the Scots. In this he promised to establish Presbyterianism in England for three years and suppress the Independents in return for immediate military help "upon the issuing of the said Declarations, that an army shall be sent from Scotland into England, for preservation and establishment of religion, for defence of His Majesty's person and authority, and restoring him to his government, to the just rights of the Crown and his full revenues (98)."

The Engagement

69

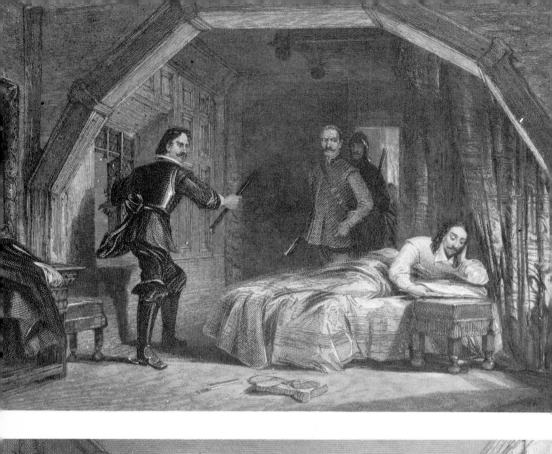

4 The Second Civil War

THE ENGLISH PARLIAMENT soon learned that some agreement had been made. It passed the Vote of No Addresses which declared:

"1. That the Lords and Commons do declare that they will make no further addresses or applications to the King.

"2. That no application or addresses be made to the King by any person whatsoever, without the leave of both Houses.

"3. That the person or persons that shall make breach of this order shall incur the penalties of high treason.

"4. That the two Houses declare they will receive no more any message from the King; and do enjoin that no person whatsoever do presume to receive or bring any message from the King to both or either of the Houses of Parliament, or to any other person (99)."

Cromwell's relief at the news can be sensed in this letter he wrote to Hammond telling of Parliament's action: "Blessed be God! I can write and thou receive freely. Dear Robin, this business hath been, I trust, a mighty providence to this poor Kingdom and to us all. The House of Commons is very sensible of the King's dealings—and of our Brethren's!—in this late transaction. You should do well, if you have anything that may discover juggling, to search it out, and let me know it. It may be of admirable use at this time, because we shall, I hope, instantly go upon business in relation to them, tending to prevent danger (100)." *Cromwell's relief*

Royalists in England believed that the time was ripe for a rising in favour of the King. One of them wrote to the Earl of Lanerick in Scotland towards the end of March, 1648: "If you intend to settle things here, you shall never do it so well as at the head of an army in England, with swords in your hands, the sight of which will only bring these to reason. The King is well and merry, though in a very straight custody (101)." *Royalist hopes*

71

Opposite, above King Charles being held prisoner in Carisbrooke Castle, Isle of Wight. *Below* Charles at conference with Parliament's commissioners

Charles tried—without success—to escape from Carisbrooke
Castle that spring, as Cromwell described in a letter to Hammond: "Intelligence came to the hands of a very considerable
person, That the King attempted to get out of his window; and
that he had a cord of silk with him whereby to slip down, but his
breast was so big the bar would not give him passage. This was
done in one of the dark nights about a fortnight ago. A gentleman
with you led him the way, and slipped down. The guard, that
night, had some quantity of wine with them (102)."

Windsor Prayer
Meeting
The second Civil War broke out in February; it consisted of
Royalist risings in Wales, Kent and Essex and a Scottish in-
vasion. Before setting out to defeat the insurgents, most of the
army leaders met at Windsor for three days of prayer and
consultation at the end of which they solemnly undertook "To
call Charles Stuart, that Man of Blood, to an account for that
blood he had shed and mischief he had done, to his utmost,
against the Lord's cause and people in these poor nations (103)."

The army's
anger
In crushing the Royalists, the army leaders showed their anger.
After General Ireton had captured Colchester, he ordered the
leading insurgents to be shot, telling them: "Know yourself—
as all others that engage a second time against the Parliament—
are traitors and rebels, and they do employ us as soldiers by
authority from them to suppress and destroy. Would you know
our commission, it's that (104)."

"Man of Blood"
The army's anger mounted when it learned that Parliament,
taking advantage of the fighting, had decided to reopen talks
with Charles, and sent commissioners to meet him at Newport
in the Isle of Wight. Colonel Thomas Harrison expressed this
mood in angry Biblical language: "Come out, come out, thou
Man of Blood. The Lord hath returned upon thee all the blood
of the house of Saul in whose stead thou hast reigned. Thou art
taken in thy mischief because thou art a Man of Blood (105)."

Remonstrance
of the Army
On 18th November, 1648, a council of officers presented to
Parliament the "Remonstrance of the Army", which demanded
that Charles I should be brought to trial: "That the capital and
grand author of our troubles, the person of the King, by whose
commissions, commands or procurement, and in whose behalf,
and for whose interest only, all our wars and troubles have been,

with all the miseries attending them, may be speedily brought to justice, for the treason, blood and mischief he's therein guilty of (106)."

When Cromwell, who had been campaigning in the north, heard of the Remonstrance, he wrote from his camp near Pontefract in Yorkshire to Thomas Fairfax, the army's commander-in-chief, in language of menacing significance: "I find in the officers of the regiments a very great sense of the sufferings of this poor kingdom; and in them all a very great zeal to have impartial justice done upon offenders. And I must confess, I do in all, from my heart, concur with them (107)." *Cromwell in sympathy*

When Charles heard of the Remonstrance, he realized what it meant, but he expressed himself calmly in a letter to his son: "This may be the last time we may speak to you or the world publicly. We are sensible into what hands we are fallen; and yet (we bless God) we have those inward refreshments the malice of our enemies cannot perturb; we have learned to busy ourself in retiring into ourself, and therefore can the better digest what befalls, not doubting but God's Providence will restrain our enemies' power and turn their fierceness to his praise (108)." *The King's calmness*

What *would* happen to the King? Cromwell's influence in the army was now so great that his decision on this issue was vital, but he had yet to make it public. Indeed, in a letter to Hammond he wished that the Remonstrance had not appeared when it did, and hoped to delay taking action: "We in this Northern Army were in a waiting posture, desiring to see what the Lord would lead us to . . . yet seeing it is come out, we trust to rejoice in the will of the Lord, waiting his further pleasure (109)." *Cromwell's indecision*

This preference for awaiting guidance before making a decision was typical of Cromwell. Earlier he had said: "If thou wilt seek to know the mind of God in all that chain of Providence, laying aside thy fleshly reason, seek of the Lord to teach thee what it is; and He will do it (110)." *Awaiting guidance*

By now the talks between Charles and Parliament had come to nothing. Neither he nor the Presbyterians would make any concessions. On 28th November the Parliamentary commissioners took leave of the King at Newport to report to Westminster. Charles knew the army would not let them return. He made a *A solemn farewell*

73

74

THIS HOVSE IS TO LET

This is an Oule

75

A contemporary print showing Cromwell expelling members from the House of Commons

solemn farewell: "My Lords, you are come to take your leave of me, and I believe we shall scarce ever see each other again; but God's will be done. I thank God, I have made my peace with him, and shall without fear undergo what he shall be pleased to suffer men to do unto me.

"My Lords, you cannot but know that, in my fall and ruin, you see your own, and that also near to you. I pray God send you better friends than I have found. I am fully informed of the whole carriage of the plot against me and mine, and nothing so much afflicts me as the sense and feeling I have of the sufferings of my subjects, and the miseries that hang over my three kingdoms drawn upon them by those who, upon pretence of public good, violently pursue their own interests and ends (111)."

The army's action   Two days later General Ireton took drastic action. Charles was removed from the Isle of Wight to Hurst Castle, a small Tudor fortress on the other side of the Solent; but still Cromwell did not speak definitely. In sending Fairfax petitions for justice from the regiments stationed in the north, he wrote in his usual uncertain way, "I verily think and am persuaded they are things which God puts into our hearts. I shall not need to offer anything to your Excellency: I know God teaches you ... I hold it my duty, having received these petitions and letters, and being desired by the framers thereof, to present them to you. The good Lord work his will upon your heart enabling you to it; and the presence of the Almighty God go along with you (112)."

Charles confident   Charles felt sure that, as King, he could not be brought to trial by any legal means. He jotted down a comment on the Remonstrance which showed the attitude he was to maintain for the rest of his life: "By the letter of the law, all persons charged to offend against the law ought to be tried by their peers or equals. What is the law, if the person questioned is without a peer? And if the law seems to condemn him, by what power shall judgment be given and who shall give it? (113)"

The army and Parliament   Parliament rejected the Remonstrance, and proposed to reopen negotiations with Charles. Again the army struck. It marched on London itself and occupied Westminster. On the evening of 5th December a meeting of officers and a few Independent members of Parliament decided that "the measures taken by the Parliament were contrary to the trust reposed in them, and tending to contract the guilt of the blood that had been shed, upon themselves and the nation . . . It was therefore the duty of the army to endeavour to put a stop to such proceedings; having engaged in the war, not simply as mercenaries, but out of judgment and conscience, being convinced that the cause in which they were engaged was just, and that the good of the people was involved in it (114)."

The next day one Colonel Pride, with a troop of musketeers, *The Rump* barred the door of the House of Commons and allowed only *Parliament* some fifty Independent members to enter. This small remnant of the Long Parliament was rudely nicknamed the Rump. The army was now completely in control of Parliament, and the capital.

A royalist writer lamented, "I could not but weep over Whitehall, when I beheld that royal mansion of our most gracious sovereign made a cage of unclean birds, but when I beheld [St.] Paul's, the royal palace of the King of Kings, the presence chamber of the living God, and His declared house of prayer, turned into a den of thieves, I could but not wish myself dissolved into tears, that I might wash away the pollution thereof (115)."

Cromwell now came to London himself. He agreed that the *Cromwell and* King should be put on trial, but he could not yet bring himself *the Levellers* to support a sentence of death (rather than deposition or exile), largely because the Levellers insisted upon death. A contemporary wrote: "I have been assured that Cromwell is retreating from [the Levellers], his designs and theirs being incompatible as fire and water, they driving at a pure democracy and himself at an oligarchy (116)."

Shortly before Christmas Day, however, Cromwell abandoned *Final decision* all hesitation. In typical fashion, he said: "If any man had deliberately designed such a thing, he would be the greatest traitor in the world, but the Providence of God had cast it upon them (117)."

Charles had now been taken to Windsor Castle. An illicit *The King's* broadsheet was on sale in the streets of London; it contained *declaration* a dignified declaration from him that he was blameless, and that

The Rump and dreggs of the house
of Com remaining after the good
members were purged out.

A satirical view of the Rump Parliament after Colonel Pride's Purge,
from a contemporary playing card

he was resigned to God's will: "There is nothing that can more obstruct the long hoped for peace of this nation, than the illegal proceedings of them that presume from servants to become masters and labour to bring in democracy . . . I once more declare unto all my loving subjects (and God knows whether or not this may be my last) that I have earnestly laboured for peace, and that my thoughts were serene and absolute, without any sinister ends, and there was nothing left undone by me, that my conscience would permit me to do . . . (118)"

Another ballad sold in the streets of London mocked the idea *Street ballad* of majority rule, the opposing claims of the sects, and the rumours about the King's fate (119):

> *Now thanks to the Powers below*
> *We have even done our do,*
> *The Mitre is down and so is the Crown*
> *And with them the Coronet too . . .*
> *There is no such thing, as a Bishop or King,*
> *Or Peer but in name or show.*
> *Come clowns and come boys, come hobbledehoys,*
> *Come females and each degree,*
> *Stretch out your throats, bringing in your votes,*
> *And make good the anarchy . . .*
> *We are fourscore religions strong,*
> *Then take your choice, the major voice*
> *Shall carry it, right or wrong;*
> *Then let's have King Charles, says George,*
> *Nay, we'll have his son, says Hugh,*
> *Nay, then let's have none, says jabbering Joan,*
> *Nay, we'll all be Kings, says Prue.*

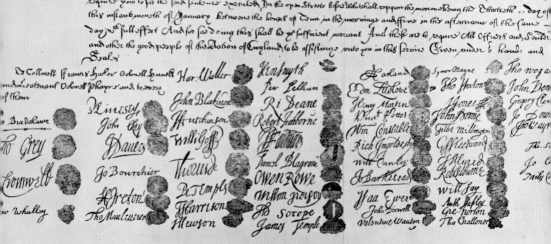

Above Charles being insulted by Cromwell's soldiers
Below Charles's death warrant

5 The King's Trial

THE RUMP passed an Act to create a special High Court of Justice for the King's Trial on 6th January, 1649: "Whereas it is notorious that Charles Stuart, the now King of England . . . hath had a wicked design totally to subvert the ancient and fundamental laws and liberties of this nation and in their place to introduce an arbitrary and tyrannical government, and that, besides all other evil ways and means to bring this design to pass, he hath prosecuted it with fire and sword, levied and maintained a cruel war in the land against the parliament and kingdom . . .

"For prevention therefore . . . and to the end [no-one] may hereafter presume traitorously and maliciously to imagine or contrive the enslaving or destroying of the English nation, and to expect impunity for so doing; be it ordained and enacted by the Commons in Parliament, and it is hereby ordained and enacted by the authority thereof, that Thomas Lord Fairfax, Oliver Cromwell, Henry Ireton [and others] shall be and are hereby appointed and required to be commissioners and judges for the hearing, trying, and adjudging of the said Charles Stuart (120)."

In all about 150 judges were appointed to sit in the High Court. Clarendon described what sort of men they were: "All the chief officers of the army were named and divers accepted the office; and such aldermen and citizens of London, as had been most violent against peace, and some few country gentlemen, whose zeal had been taken notice of for the cause, and who were like to take such a preferment as a testimony of the parliament's confidence in them, and would thereupon embrace it (121)."

John Bradshaw, a barrister, was appointed President of the High Court. Clarendon gave this account of him. (For centuries Westminster Hall had been the meeting-place of the ordinary law courts, and in it were also held great state trials): "Bradshaw

83

Charles with his secretary, Sir Edward Walker

was chosen, a lawyer of Gray's inn, not much known in Westminster Hall, though of good practice in his chamber, and much employed by the factious and discontented persons. He was a gentleman of an ancient family in Cheshire and Lancashire, but of a fortune of his own making. He was not without parts and of great insolence and ambition (122)."

Lack of due respect

Charles was brought by coach from Windsor Castle on 19th January to London. There he was lodged in St. James's Palace and no longer treated with the respect due to royalty. Clarendon sadly related: "From the time of the King's being come to St. James's, . . . his majesty was treated with more rudeness and barbarity than he had ever been before. No man was suffered to see or speak to him, but the soldiers who were his guard, some of whom sat up always in his bedchamber, and drank and took tobacco, as if they had been upon the court of guard; nor was he suffered to go into any other room, either to say his prayers, or to receive the ordinary benefits of nature, but was obliged to do both in their presence and before them (123)."

Mood of the army

The next day the Army Council redrafted the Agreement of the People and presented it to the Rump Parliament. The army was ready to impose the death penalty on others as well as the King: "It is agreed, that whosoever shall, by force of arms, resist the orders of the next or any future Representative (except in case where such Representative shall evidently render up, or give, or take away the foundations of common right, liberty, and safety, contained in this Agreement), he shall forthwith, after his or their such resistance, lose the benefit and protection of the laws, and shall be punishable with death, as an enemy and traitor to the nation (124)."

Cromwell forthright

Ever since 8th January the Commissioners for the King's Trial had been meeting in the Painted Chamber, the former royal bedchamber of the ancient Palace of Westminster. Only about half of those named had accepted their appointment. Many of those present doubted their right to try the King. But with characteristic scorn of constitutional problems, Cromwell remarked, "I tell you, we will cut off his head with the crown upon it (125)."

Nevertheless, the question of the Court's authority was

important. A Royalist gentleman, who claimed to have hidden in the Painted Chamber, said that the Commissioners were still at a loss for an answer on the morning of 20th January, the day when the trial was due to begin. *By what authority?*

As they deliberated, news was brought that Charles had been brought by boat along the River Thames to Westminster: "At which Cromwell ran to the window, looking on the King as he came up the garden. He turned as white as the wall . . . then turning to the board said thus: 'My masters, he is come, he is come, and now we are doing that great work that the whole nation will be full of. Therefore I desire you to let us resolve here what answer we shall give the King when he comes before us, for the first question he will ask us will be by what authority and commission we do try him?' For a time no one answered. Then after a little space, Henry Marten rose up and said, 'In the name of the Commons in Parliament assembled and all the good people of England' (126)."

The King's trial opened on the afternoon of Saturday, 20th January in Westminster Hall. It began with the reading of the names of the Commissioners, as described by Clarendon: "There was an accident happened that first day, which may be fit to be remembered. When all those who were Commissioners had taken their places, and the King was brought in, the first ceremony was to read their commission, which was the ordinance of Parliament for the trial . . . Then the judges were all called, every man answering to his name as he was called, and the president being first called and making answer, the next who was called being the general, Lord Fairfax, and no answer being made, the officer called him the second time, when there was a voice heard that said, 'he had more wit than to be there'; which put the court into some disorder, and somebody asking, who it was, there was no answer but a little murmuring (127)." *The trial begins*

It was Lady Fairfax who shouted out from the gallery; and when the list was completed, it was found that only 68 of the 135 Commissioners were present.

Charles was then brought in and placed at a seat opposite Bradshaw. As Lord President of the Court, Bradshaw opened the proceedings: "Charles Stuart, King of England, the Commons of *Bradshaw*

England assembled in Parliament being deeply sensible of the calamities that have been brought upon this nation, which is fixed upon you as the principal author of it, have resolved to make inquisition for blood; and according to that debt and duty they owe to justice, to God, the kingdom, and themselves, and according to the fundamental power that rests in themselves, they have resolved to bring you to trial and judgement: and for that purpose have constituted this High Court of Justice, before which you are brought (128)."

The charge John Cook, the Solicitor for the Commonwealth, immediately followed with the charge against the King. This accused him of ruling as a tyrant and waging war against the Parliament and people. It concluded: "The said Charles Stuart hath been, and is the occasioner, author, and continuer of the said unnatural cruel and bloody wars; and therein guilty of all the treasons, murders, rapines, burnings, spoils, desolations, damages and mischiefs to this nation, acted and committed in the said wars, or occasioned thereby (129)."

A significant incident Charles wanted to interrupt Cook. He tried to tap him with the silver-headed cane that he always carried, but: "As the charge was reading against the King, the head of his staff fell off, which he wondered at; and seeing none to take it up, he stoops for it himself (130)." This incident made Charles realize that he was no longer being treated as a king since no one was waiting on him.

The King's answer When the charge had been read, Bradshaw addressed the King, "Sir, you have now heard your charge; the Court expects your answer." Charles had never been a good speaker, but his reply was fluent and clear: "Remember I am your King, your *lawful* King, and what sins you bring upon your heads, and the judgment of God upon this land; think well upon it, I say, think well upon it, before you go from one sin to a greater . . . I have a trust committed to me by God, by old and lawful descent. I will not betray it to answer a new unlawful authority. Therefore resolve me that and you shall hear more of me (131)."

The nature of kingship To this challenge, Bradshaw replied by urging Charles to answer "in the name of the people of England, of which you are *elected* King." This was contrary to Charles I's belief in the

A Puritan propaganda cartoon, showing atrocities supposedly committed
by the Royalists

divine nature of his position. It was also contrary to the facts;
and he stated with conviction: "England was never an elective
kingdom, but an hereditary kingdom for near these thousand
years; therefore let me know by what authority I am called
hither: I do stand more for the liberty of my people than any
here that come to be my pretended judges (132)."

To this there was no real reply. Bradshaw now sought to
rebuke the King for his attitude towards the Court: "Sir, how
really you have managed your trust, is known: your way of
answer is to interrogate the Court which beseems not you in this
condition. You have been told of it twice or thrice (133)."

*The King
rebuked*

87

Charles was not to be silenced. He went on to assert the illegality of the Court, which had been set up by the Rump alone: "I do not come here as submitting to the Court: I will stand as much for the privilege of the House of Commons, rightly understood, as any man here whatsoever. I see no House of Lords here that may constitute a Parliament ... Let me see a legal authority warranted by the Word of God, the Scriptures, or warranted by the constitution of the kingdom, and I will answer (134)."

Bradshaw decided that the only way to interrupt Charles was to bring the day's proceedings to an end, and order the King to be removed. This was evidently the pre-arranged sign for a demonstration by the soldiers in the Hall, who shouted, "Justice! Justice!" Charles seemed to be taken by surprise by this, and Bradshaw changed his plan and suddenly repeated his demand for the King's answer to the charge.

Charles immediately recovered himself and began another long speech: "Let me tell you, it is not a slight thing you are about. I am sworn to keep the peace, by that duty I owe to God and my country, and I will do it to the last breath of my body; and therefore you shall do well to satisfy first God, and then the country, by what authority you do it; if you do it by an usurped authority you cannot answer. There is a God in Heaven, that will call you, and all that give you power, to account (135)."

At last Bradshaw was able to break into the King's discourse, and the Court was adjourned after the following exchange:

Lord President: "The Court expects you should give them a final answer. Their purpose is to adjourn to Monday next. If you do not satisfy yourself, though we do tell you our authority, and it is upon God's authority and the kingdom; and that peace you speak of will be kept in the doing of justice, and that is our present work."

King: "For answer, let me tell you, you have shown no lawful authority to satisfy any reasonable man."

Lord President: "That is, in your apprehension. We are satisfied that are your judges."

King: "It is not my apprehension, nor yours neither, that ought to decide it."

Lord President: "The Court hath heard you, and you are to be disposed of as they have commanded (136)." *Charles led away*

After defiantly noting the sword of state, which lay on the Lord President's table, Charles was taken away. The royal prisoner had a mixed reception from the soldiers and spectators: "As the King went away, facing the Court, he said, 'I do not fear that' (meaning the sword). The people in the Hall, as he went down the stairs, cried out, some 'God save the King', and most for 'Justice' (137)."

Clarendon described how the crowd behaved towards the King. Many seemed to be enraged by his defiance of the Court: "As there was in many persons present at that woeful spectacle a real duty and compassion for the King, so there was in others so barbarous and brutal a behaviour towards him, that they called him tyrant and murderer; and one spit in his face; which his majesty, without expressing any trouble, wiped off with his handkerchief (138)." *Attitude of the crowd*

The Court did not sit the next day, since it was a Sunday. Charles wrote a statement which he hoped to make at the next sitting, but he was not to be allowed to do this. He insisted that in challenging the Court, he was defending the liberty of the English people: "The duty I owe to God in the preservation of the true liberty of my people will not suffer me at this time to be silent: for, how can any free-born subject of England call life or anything he possesseth his own, if power without right daily make new, and abrogate the old fundamental laws of the land which I now take to be the present case? (139)." *Preservation of liberty*

He defied the Court to show how it could possibly be lawful: "The law upon which you ground your proceedings must either be old or new. If old, show it. If new, tell what authority, warranted by the fundamental laws of the land, hath made it, and when. But how the House of Commons can erect a Court of Judicature, which was never one itself (as is well known to all lawyers) I leave to God and the world to judge. And it were full as strange, that they should pretend to make laws without King or Lords' House, to any that have heard speak of the laws of England (140)." *An unlawful Court*

Charles attacked the idea that the Court represented the

89

wishes of the English people. Even if "the people of England's commission could grant your pretended power, I see nothing you can show for that; for certainly you never asked the question of the tenth man in the kingdom, and in this way you manifestly wrong even the poorest ploughman, if you demand not his free consent. Nor can you pretend any colour for this your pretended commission, without the consent at least of the major part of every man in England . . . which I am sure you never went about to seek, so far are you from having it (141)."

He believed that the peace of the country was at stake: "The peace of the kingdom is not the least in my thoughts; and what hope of settlement is there, so long as power reigns without rule or law, changing the whole frame of that government under which this kingdom hath flourished for many hundred years? (142)."

When the Court resumed on Monday, 22nd January, steps were taken to prevent any protest such as Lady Fairfax had made at the last sitting. The official report noted: "*O Yes!* made; silence commanded; the Court called, and answered to their names. Silence commanded upon pain of imprisonment, and the Captain of the Guard to apprehend all such as make disturbance. Upon the King's coming in a shout was made. Command given by the Court to the Captain of the Guard, to fetch and take into his custody those who make any disturbance (143)."

Cook was slow to begin the proceedings, but Charles did not wish to be kept waiting. He poked Cook with his cane. Cook glared at him and began: "May it please your lordship, my Lord President, I did at the last Court in the behalf of the Commons of England exhibit and give in to this Court a charge of high treason and other high crimes against the prisoner at the bar . . . My lord, he was not then pleased to give an answer, but instead of answering did there dispute the authority of this High Court. My humble motion . . . is that the prisoner may be directed to make a positive answer either by way of confession or negation; which if he shall refuse to do, that the matter of the charge may be taken *pro confesso*, and the Court may proceed according to justice (144)."

91

The chair in which King Charles sat throughout his trial

Bradshaw supported Cook in this threat, that if the King would not answer the charge, he should be regarded as having admitted his guilt. Charles was not overawed. Without speaking from notes, he showed that setting out his ideas on paper over the weekend had enabled him to show up clearly the weakness of the Court's position:

"If it were only my own particular case, I would have satisfied myself with the protestation I made the last time I was here against the legality of this Court, and that a king cannot be tried by any superior jurisdiction on earth. But it is not my case alone, it is the freedom and the liberty of the people of England; and do you pretend what you will, I stand more for their liberties. For if the power without law may make laws, may alter the fundamental laws of the kingdom, I do not know what subject he is in England, that can be sure of his life, or anything that he calls his own (145)."

Bradshaw quickly cut him short, saying that the Court could not listen to the arguments of a delinquent; he demanded from him "a punctual and direct answer"; but Charles answered ironically polite:

King: "Sir, by your favour, I do not know the forms of law; I do know law and reason, though I am no lawyer professed; but I know as much law as any gentleman in England; and therefore under favour I do plead for the liberties of the people of England more than you do: and therefore if I should impose a belief upon any man, without reasons given for it, it were unreasonable. But I must tell you, that that reason that I have, as thus informed, I cannot yield unto it."

Lord President: "Sir, I must interrupt you, you may not be permitted. You speak of law and reason; it is fit there should be law and reason, and there is both against you. Sir, the vote of the Commons of England assembled in Parliament, it is the reason of the kingdom, and they are these that have given to that law, according to which you should have ruled and reigned. Sir, you are not to dispute our authority, you are told it again by the Court. Sir, it will be taken notice of, that you stand in contempt of the Court, and your contempt will be recorded accordingly (146)."

Since he was already charged with murder and treason, Charles paid little attention to the threat of contempt of court. He insisted that any accused person had the right to show why he questioned the capacity of a court. Bradshaw could only bluster in reply:

King: "I do not know how a King can be a delinquent, but by any law that ever I heard of, all men (delinquents, or what you will), let me tell you, they may put in demurrers against any proceeding as legal—and I do demand that, and demand to be heard with my reasons. If you deny that, you deny reason."

Lord President: "Sir, you have offered something unto you, the sense of the Court. Sir, neither you nor any man are permitted to dispute that point. You are concluded, you may not demur to the jurisdiction of the Court. If you do, I must let you know, that they overrule your demurrer. They sit here by the authority of the Commons of England, and all your predecessors and you are responsible and you are responsible to them (147)."

Charles was still not to be silenced. He added that, although Parliament was a court, the House of Commons alone was not:

King: "I deny that; show me one precedent."

Lord President: "Sir, you ought not to interrupt while the Court is speaking to you. This point is not to be debated by you, neither will the Court permit you to do it: if you offer it by way of demurrer to the jurisdiction of the Court, they have considered of their jurisdiction, they do affirm their own jurisdiction."

King: "I say, Sir, by your favour, that the Commons of England was never a Court of Judicature; I would know how they came to be so (148)."

In desperation, Bradshaw ordered the clerk of the Court to call upon Charles to answer the charge: "Charles Stuart, King of England, you have been accused on behalf of the people of England of high treason, and other high crimes. The Court have determined that you ought to answer the same (149)."

When Charles remained defiant, Bradshaw could only end the sitting of the Court by ordering the guards to take the King away. But Charles refused to leave:

King: "I will answer the same as soon as I know by what

authority you do this."

Lord President: "If this be all that you will say, then, gentlemen, you that brought the prisoner hither, take charge of him back again."

King: "I do require that I may give in my reasons why I do not answer, and give me time for that."

Lord President: "Sir, it is not for prisoners to require."

King: "Prisoners! Sir, I am not an ordinary prisoner (150)."

Threat to the King

When Charles persisted, Bradshaw threatened that the next sitting of the Court would be the last:

King: "Show me that jurisdiction where reason is not to be heard."

Lord President: "Sir, we show it you here, the Commons of England, and the next time you are brought, you will know more of the pleasure of the Court, and, it may be, their final determination (151)."

Laws and liberties

After a final exchange, the sitting ended with Charles still trying to make himself heard as the guards took him away:

King: "Well, Sir, remember that the King is not suffered to give in his reasons for the liberty and freedom of all his subjects."

Lord President: "Sir, you are not to have liberty to use this language. How great a friend you have been to the laws and liberties of the people, let all England and the world judge."

King: "Sir, under favour, it was the liberty, freedom, and laws of the subject that ever I took—defended myself with arms; I never took up arms against the people, but for the laws (152)."

Verdict of guilty

Cook reopened the proceedings on Tuesday, 23rd January. He began by insisting that the King was guilty: "The House of Commons, the supreme authority and jurisdiction of the kingdom, they have declared, that it is notorious, that the matter of the charge is true, as it is in truth, my lord, as clear as crystal and as the sun that shines at noonday: which if your lordship and the Court be not satisfied in, I have notwithstanding, on the people of England's behalf, several witnesses to produce . . . And therefore I do humbly pray that speedy judgment be pronounced against the prisoner at the bar (153)."

One last chance

94

Bradshaw came next. He claimed that the Court would be justified in sentencing Charles without delay. But he gave him one more opportunity: "Sir, in plain terms, for justice knows no respect of persons; you are to give your positive and final answer in plain English, whether you be guilty or not guilty of these treasons laid to your charge (154)."

After a pause, Charles replied: "When I was here yesterday, I did desire to speak for the liberties of the people of England. I was interrupted. I desire to know yet whether I may speak freely or not (155)." *Freely or not*

Bradshaw stated that the Court would hear him "make the best defence you can," but only if he answered "the matter that is charged upon you." Charles contemptuously ignored him and again asserted his authority: *The King's authority*

"For the charge, I value it not a rush; it is the liberty of the people of England that I stand for. For me to acknowledge a new court, that I never heard of before, I that am your King, that should be an example to all the people of England, for to uphold justice, to maintain the old laws; indeed I do not know how to do it. You spoke very well the first day that I came here (on Saturday) of the obligations that I had laid upon me by God, to the maintenance of the liberties of my people; the same obligation you spake of, I do acknowledge to God that I owe to Him, and to my people, to defend as much as in me lies the ancient laws of the kingdom: therefore, until that I may know that this is not against the fundamental laws of the kingdom, by your favour I can put in no particular charge. If you will give me time, I will show you my reasons why I cannot do it, and this—— (156)."

The final word in his last complete sentence should have been "answer", but by a slip of the tongue he said "charge"— probably because he thought that he should have been able to charge the members of the Court with treason.

When Bradshaw tried again to interrupt him, the King was not to be silenced, but went on to refer to the talks which he had had with Parliament: "By your favour, you ought not to interrupt me. How I came here, I know not. There's no law for it to make your King your prisoner. I was in a treaty upon the public faith of the kingdom, that was the known—two Houses of Parliament that was the representatives of the kingdom; *Interruption ignored*

and when I had almost made an end of the Treaty, then I was hurried away, and brought hither: and therefore —— (157)."

Bradshaw then said, "Sir, you must know the pleasure of the Court": *Scornful comment*

King: "By your favour, Sir."

Lord President: "Nay, Sir, by your favour, you may not be permitted to fall into those discourses; you appear as a delinquent, you have not acknowledged the authority of the Court, the Court craves it not of you; but once more they command you to give your positive answer. Clerk, do your duty."

King: "Duty, Sir! (158)"

Bradshaw could only quieten the King by calling on the clerk to repeat for the last time the formal demand for the King's answer, but he could not prevent a scornful comment from Charles.

The clerk hurriedly read out the charge once more: "Charles *The charge* Stuart, King of England, you are accused in behalf of the *repeated* Commons of England of divers crimes and treasons, which charge hath been read unto you; the Court now requires you to give your positive and final answer, by way of confession or denial of the charge (159)."

Charles's only reply was again to deny the legality of the *The sitting* Court, in the interests, he insisted, of the English people. *ended* Bradshaw brought the sitting to an end: "How far you have preserved the privileges of the people, your actions have spoke it. But truly, Sir, men's intentions ought to be known by their actions. You have written your meaning in bloody characters throughout the whole kingdom. But, Sir, you understand the pleasure of the Court—Clerk, record the default—and, gentlemen, you that took charge of the prisoner, take him back again (160)."

So the third session of the Court ended with this final threat *A final threat* from Bradshaw and a dry comment by Charles:

Lord President: "Sir, you have heard the pleasure of the Court, and you are (notwithstanding you will not understand it) to find that you are before a court of justice."

King: "I see I am before a power (161)."

Since Charles was reckoned to have pleaded guilty, witnesses

Opposite Charles sits facing the Commissioners during his trial. A print from the *True Copy of the Journal of the High Court of Justice for the Tryal of King Charles I* (1684)

could not be called by the Court. But, to satisfy the public about the strength of their case the Commissioners spent all Wednesday and Thursday in the Painted Chamber hearing evidence, mostly from soldiers, that the King had taken part in the Civil War.

On Thursday the Court "Resolved upon the whole matter: that this Court will proceed to sentence of Condemnation against Charles Stuart, King of England ... That the condemnation of the King shall be for a tyrant, traitor and murderer ... That the condemnation of the King shall be likewise for being a public enemy to the Commonwealth of England ... That this condemnation *shall extend to death* (162)."

When the Court resumed on Saturday, 27th January, Charles did not wait for the Lord President to open the proceedings, but began at once: "I shall desire a word to be heard a little, and I hope I shall give no occasion of interruption (163)."

Bradshaw was determined that the King should not speak first. After some argument Charles gave way on the understanding that he would be heard later, and Bradshaw began his speech to the Court: "Gentlemen, it is well known to all, or most of you here present, that the prisoner at the bar hath been several times convened and brought before the Court to make answer to a charge of treason, and other high crimes exhibited against him in the name of the people of England—— (164)."

At this moment a masked lady in one of the galleries shouted out: "Not half, not a quarter of the people of England! Oliver Cromwell is a traitor! (165)."

It was Lady Fairfax again. Clarendon described the incident: "Upon which, one of the officers bid the soldiers give fire into that box whence those presumptuous words were uttered. But it was quickly discerned that it was the general's wife, the lady Fairfax, who had uttered both those sharp sayings; who was presently persuaded or forced to leave the place, to prevent any new disorder (166)."

When silence had been restored, the Lord President went on with his speech. He stated that the Court had fully considered the case; since the prisoner had not pleaded, he must be regarded as having confessed; and since the charges brought against him were notorious, its members had agreed upon the sentence, but were still willing to hear him speak in his defence before pronouncing it, as long as he did not "offer any debate" about the Court's powers.

Charles attempted no debate, but carefully repeated his attitude towards the Court: "Since that I see that you will not hear anything of debate concerning that which I confess I thought most material for the peace of the kingdom and for the liberty of the subject, I shall waive it. I shall speak nothing to it, but only I must tell you, that this many a day all things have been taken away from me, but that, that I call more dear to me than my life, which is my conscience and my honour. And if I had respect to my life more than the peace of the Kingdom and the liberty of the subject, certainly I should have made a particular defence for myself; for by that at leastwise I might have delayed an ugly sentence, which I believe will pass upon me...

"Now, sir, I conceive, that an hasty sentence once passed, may sooner be repented than recalled. And truly, the self-same desire that I have for the peace of the kingdom, and the liberty of the subject ... does make me now [desire] before sentence be given, that I may be heard in the Painted Chamber before the Lords and Commons ...

"I do conjure you, as you love that which you pretend (I hope it is real) the liberty of the subject and the peace of the kingdom, that you will grant me the hearing, before any sentence be passed ... If I cannot get this liberty, I do here protest that so fair shows of liberty and peace, are pure shows and not otherwise, since you will not hear your King (167)."

Charles's words produced a disturbance among the Commissioners. One of them, John Downes, protested so violently that Bradshaw had to suspend the sitting of the Court: *The Court suspended*

Downes: "Have we hearts of stone? Are we men?"

Cromwell: "What ails thee? Art thout mad? Canst thou not sit still and be quiet?"

Downes: "Sir, no, I cannot be quiet. If I die for it, I must do it. I am not satisfied to give my consent to the sentence. I desire the Court may adjourn to hear my reasons (168)."

The Commissioners argued for half an hour outside the Hall.

101

Lady Fairfax, in one of the galleries, declaring Oliver Cromwell a traitor

A contract broken Cromwell called Charles "the hardest-hearted man on earth," and Downes a "peevish, tenacious fellow". Eventually, Downes was silenced. When the Court resumed, Bradshaw delivered his final speech which lasted forty minutes. He accused the King of breaking his contract with his people:

"There is a contract and a bargain made between the King and his people, and your oath is taken: and certainly, Sir, the bond is reciprocal: for as you are the liege lord, so they liege subjects . . . This we know now, the one tie, the one bond, is the bond of protection that is due from the sovereign; the other is the bond of subjection that is due from the subject. Sir, if this bond be once broken, farewell sovereignty! These things may not be denied, Sir . . .

"Whether you have been, as by your office you ought to be, a protector of England, or the destroyer of England, let all England judge, or all the world that hath look'd upon in (169)."

Violent words Bradshaw went on to repeat the charge in violent language: "Sir, the charge hath called you a Tyrant, a Traitor, a Murderer, and a public enemy to the Commonwealth of England. Sir, it had been well if that any of all these terms might rightly and justly have been spared, if any one of them at all.

"Though we should not be delivered from those bloody hands and hearts that conspire the overthrow of the kingdom in general, and of us in particular for acting in this great work of justice, though we should perish in the work, yet by God's grace and by God's strength, we will go on with it (170)."

Charles angered When Bradshaw urged the King to implore God's forgiveness for blood-guiltiness, as David did for the death of Uriah, Charles angrily broke in:

King: "I would desire only one word before you give sentence; and that is that you would hear me concerning those great imputations that you have laid to my charge."

Lord President: "Truly, Sir, I would not willingly, at this time especially, interrupt you in anything you have to say that is proper for us to admit of. But, Sir, you have not owned us as a Court, and you look upon us as a sort of people met together; and we knew what language we receive from your party."

102 *King:* "I know nothing of that."

Lord President: "You disavow us as a Court: and therefore for you to address yourself to us, not acknowledging us as a Court to judge of what you say, it is not to be permitted. And the truth is, all along, from the first time you were pleased to disavow and disown us, the Court needed not to have heard you one word (171)."

The clerk now read out the sentence against the King, which was drawn up on parchment: "Whereas the Commons of England in Parliament had appointed them a High Court of Justice, for the trying of Charles Stuart, King of England, before whom he had been three times convened; and at the first time a charge of high treason, and other crimes and misdemeanours was read in the behalf of the kingdom of England . . . *Sentence of death*

"Which charge being read unto him, as aforesaid, he the said Charles Stuart was required to give his answer: but he refused so to do; and so expressed the several passages of his trial in refusing to answer. For all which treasons and crimes this Court doth adjudge, that the said Charles Stuart, as a tyrant, traitor, murderer, and a public enemy, shall be put to death, by the severing his head from his body (172)."

Since a prisoner condemned to death was considered already dead in law, he was not allowed to speak after sentence. But Charles made a vain attempt to refute the imputations that had been made against him by Bradshaw in his speech: *Charles tries to speak*

King: "Will you hear me a word, Sir?"

Lord President: "Sir, you are not to be heard after the sentence."

King: "No, Sir!"

Lord President: "No, Sir; by your favour, Sir. Guard, withdraw your prisoner."

King: "I may speak after the sentence—by your favour, Sir, I may speak after the sentence ever . . . By your favour (Hold!) the sentence, Sir—— I say, Sir, I do—— I am not suffered for to speak: expect what justice other people will have (173)."

As Charles was led away from Westminster Hall, the soldiers cried out, "Execution! Justice! Execution!" He remarked with a smile: "Poor creatures, for sixpence they will say as much of their own commanders (174)." *His final remark*

104

6 The King's Execution

THE NEXT DAY was Sunday, 28th January. Hugh Peters, an Independent minister who had followed Cromwell on several campaigns, preached before the soldiers stationed in St. James's Palace. He took as his text a passage from Isaiah XIV,

"All the kings of the nations, even all of them, lie in glory, every one in his own house.

"But thou art cast out of thy grave like an abominable branch, and as the raiment of those that are slain, thrust through with a sword . . .

"Thou shalt not be joined to them in burial, because thou hast destroyed thy land and slain thy people (175)."

He wished Charles had been there to hear it, but Charles had been lodged in Whitehall Palace during the trial and was not taken back to St. James's until that afternoon.

On the Monday morning, while the carpenters were erecting the scaffold outside the Banqueting House of Whitehall Palace, the Commissioners met again in the Painted Chamber. Here, fifty-nine of them signed the King's death warrant, and directed the army officers to carry out his execution on the next day:

"Whereas Charles Stuart, King of England, is, and standeth convicted, attainted, and condemned of high treason and other high crimes; and sentence upon Saturday last was pronounced against him by this Court, to be put to death by the severing of his head from his body; of which sentence, execution yet remaineth to be done.

"These are therefore to will and require you to see the said sentence executed in the open street before Whitehall, upon the morrow, being the thirtieth day of this instant month of January, between the hours of ten in the morning and five in the afternoon of the same day, with full effect. And for so doing this shall be your sufficient warrant. And these are to require all officers,

Opposite The medal given to Bishop Juxon by Charles on the scaffold soldiers, and others, the good people of this nation of England, to be assisting unto you in this service (176)."

A farewell   Charles spent Sunday and Monday preparing himself for the end. With him was William Juxon, Bishop of London. Charles's two children in England, Princess Elizabeth and the Duke of Gloucester, were brought from Sion House to see him.

The Princess, who was thirteen, wrote down that night what he said to her: "He told me he was glad I was come, and although he had not time to say much, yet somewhat he had to say to me, which he had not to another, or have in writing, because he feared their cruelty was such, as that they would not have permitted him to write to me.

"He wished me not to grieve and torment myself for him, for that would be a glorious death that he should die, it being for the laws and liberties of this land, and for maintaining the true Protestant Religion. He bid me read Bishop Andrews' *Sermons*, Hooker's *Ecclesiastical Polity* and Bishop Laud's book against Fisher, which would ground me against Popery.

"He told me he had forgiven all his enemies, and hoped God would forgive them also, and commanded us, and all the rest of my brothers and sisters to forgive them. He bid me tell my mother that his thoughts had never strayed from her, and that his love should be the same to the last. Withal he commanded me and my brother to be obedient to her, and bid me send his blessing to the rest of my brothers and sisters, with commendation to all his friends . . .

"He commanded us all to forgive these people, but never to trust them, for they had been most false to him and to those that gave them power, and he feared also to their own souls. [He] desired me not to grieve for him, for he should die a martyr . . . He doubted not but the Lord would settle his throne upon his son, and that we should be all happier than we could have expected to have been if he had lived (177)."

Another farewell   To the Duke of Gloucester, who was eight, Charles spoke as simply as he could. He took the boy on his knee: "Mark, child, what I say. They will cut off my head, and perhaps make thee a king. But mark what I say, you must not be a king so long as your brothers Charles and James do live; for they will cut off

106

Opposite, above Charles's interview with his children, before his execution.
Below Cromwell conferring with his lawyers

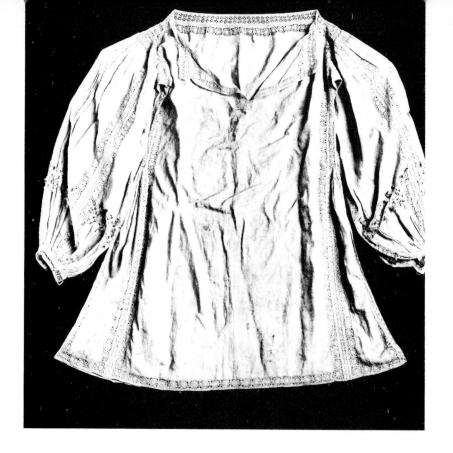

your brothers' heads (when they can catch them) and cut off thy head too, at last. And therefore I charge you, do not be made a king by them (178)."

It was important for the boy to understand this because family unity and the lawful succession to the throne were involved. Charles was pleased when the boy replied, "I will be torn to pieces first."

Charles was allowed to receive a messenger from the Prince of Wales, who was in Holland. This was Henry Seymour, who had once been a page and courtier. The Prince could do more than send his father a brief letter: "I do not only pray for Your Majesty according to my duty, but shall always be ready to do all which shall be in my power to deserve that blessing which I now humbly beg of Your Majesty (179)." *A prince's message*

The King later gave Bishop Juxon a letter for the Prince of Wales. He wrote: "The true glory of princes consists in advancing God's glory, in the maintenance of true religion and the Church's good; also in the dispensation of civil power, with justice and honour to the public peace (180)." *A letter*

Soon afterwards, the King's attendant Sir Thomas Herbert went out into the Park, and met a kinsman, George Herbert's brother, Henry. Henry sent a message that Charles would find much comfort in the second chapter of Ecclesiasticus: "For gold is tried in the fire, and acceptable men in the furnace of adversity. They that fear the Lord will prepare their hearts, and humble their souls in his sight, Saying, We will fall into the hands of the Lord and not into the hands of men: for as His Majesty is, so is His Mercy (181)." *A text of comfort*

Charles spent the rest of the evening in prayer and meditation with Bishop Juxon, and then slept from about midnight to six in the morning. On awakening he called his attendant to help him dress: "Herbert, this is my second marriage day. I would be as trim today as may be, for before night I hope to be espoused to my blessed Jesus (182)." *Preparing for death*

It was a bitterly cold morning, with frost on the ground. Charles put on two shirts in order not to shiver on the scaffold: "Let me have a shirt more than ordinary, by reason the season is so sharp as probably may make me shake, which some will *Two shirts*

109

Opposite, above One of the two shirts which Charles wore at his execution.
Below A contemporary Dutch engraving depicting the King's last days

imagine proceeds from fear. I would have no such imputation. I fear not death. I bless my God I am prepared (183)."

After receiving the Sacrament from Bishop Juxon, Charles was taken under escort at about ten o'clock to Whitehall. He had eaten nothing since the night before, but Juxon persuaded him to eat a piece of bread and drink a glass of wine.

At about half-past one he was summoned to the scaffold. The scene was described by a foreign observer: "On the scaffold the King showed a remarkable constancy. His beard was long and grey, his hair white, and he was greatly aged. The two executioners were masked and wore false beards and wigs. Upon the scaffold, which was newly draped, were iron chains and ropes to allow force to be used with the King if he did not submit of his own accord to the axe (184)."

Charles took a small piece of paper out of his pocket on which he had written a few notes and began to speak to those on the scaffold: "I shall be very little heard of anybody here ... I shall therefore speak a word unto you here. Indeed, I could hold my peace very well, but I think it is my duty to God first, and to my country, for to clear myself both as an honest man, a good King and a good Christian.

"I think it is not very needful for me to insist long upon this, for all the world knows that I never did begin a war first with the two Houses of Parliament ...

"God forbid I should lay it on the two Houses of Parliament ... I do believe that ill instruments between them and me have been the chief cause of all this bloodshed (185)."

Yet, though as a King he considered his sentence illegal, he added that as a Christian he recognized his fate as God's punishment on him. Although he did not mention Strafford by name, he clearly had him in mind: "An unjust sentence that I suffered to take effect, is punished now by an unjust sentence on me (186)."

Charles went on as a Christian to forgive his enemies: "I wish that they may repent, for indeed they have committed a great sin in that particular; I pray God, with St. Stephen, that this be not laid to their charge. Nay, not only so, but that they may take the right way to the peace of the kingdom: for my charity commands me not only to forgive particular men, but my charity commands me to endeavour to the last gasp the peace of the kingdom. So, sirs, I do wish with all my soul, (and I do hope there is some here will carry it further) that they may endeavour the peace of the kingdom (187)."

He then spoke of his people: "Truly, I desire their liberty and freedom as much as anybody whomsoever. But I must tell you their liberty and freedom consists in having of government, those laws by which their life and their goods may be most their own. It is not for having a share in government, sir, that is nothing pertaining to them. A subject and a sovereign are clear different things . . . Sirs, it was for this that now I am come here. If I would have given way to an arbitrary way, for to have all laws changed according to the power of the sword, I needed not to have come here; and therefore I tell you (and I pray God it

The martyr of the people

The King's execution, a contemporary woodcut

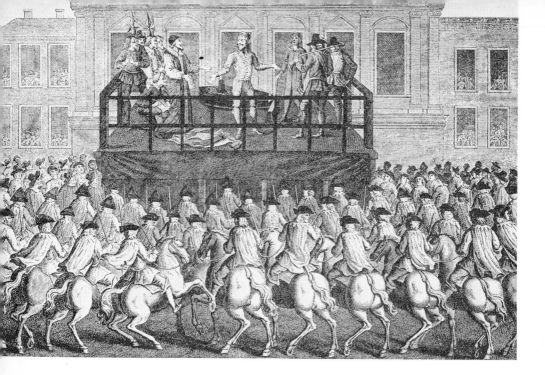

Charles addressing the crowd before his execution

be not laid to your charge) that I am the martyr of the people (188)."

Profession of faith

Charles would have ended there had not Bishop Juxon reminded him—"for the world's satisfaction"—that he should say something about his religion. And so Charles said: "I die a Christian according to the profession of the Church of England, as I found it left me by my father . . . I have a good cause and I have a gracious God; I will say no more (189)."

Juxon's last words

Juxon spoke his last words to his King: "There is but one stage more, which though turbulent and troublesome, yet it is a very short one. You may consider it will soon carry you a very great way. It will carry you from Earth to Heaven, and there you shall find, to your great joy, the prize you hasten to, a crown of Glory (190)."

The King's reply

The King answered: "I go from a corruptible to an incorruptible crown, where no disturbance can be, no disturbance in the world (191)."

Charles gave his George, the insignia of the Order of the Garter, to Juxon, took off his doublet, prayed for a moment, and placed his neck on the block. Philip Henry, then a boy of seventeen, standing in the crowd around the scaffold, saw the axe fall and never forgot the sound that accompanied it: "The blow I saw given, and can truly say, with a sad heart. At the instant whereof, I remember well, there was such a groan by the thousands there present as I never heard before, and desire I may never hear again (192)." *The final scene*

Clarendon passed his verdict on Charles: "The King himself showed a calm and composed firmness, which was more remarkable, because it was not natural, and therefore imputed to an extraordinary measure of Divine assistance. Bishop Juxon did the office of his function honestly, but too coldly to raise the King's thoughts; so that it was owing wholly to somewhat within himself that he suffered so many indignities with so much true courage, without any show of disorder, or any sort of affectation. Thus he died, greater than he lived, and verified what has been observed of the whole race of the Stuarts, that they bore misfortunes better than prosperity (193)." *The axe falls*

A spectator described the scene that followed as the huge crowd surged onto the scaffold and bought relics of their dead King from the guards: "They were inhumanly barbarous to his dead corpse. His hair and his blood were sold by parcels. Their hands and sticks were tinged by his blood and the block, now cut into chips, as also the sand sprinkled with his sacred gore, were exposed for sale. Which were greedily bought, but for different ends; by some as trophies of their slain enemy and by others as precious relics of their beloved prince (194)." *Barbarous aftermath*

Charles was buried in St. George's Chapel, Windsor, on a wintry day. Herbert recorded that when "the King's body was brought out of St. George's hall the sky was serene and clear. But presently it began to snow, and fell so fast as, by the time they came to the west end of the royal chapel, the black velvet pall was all white (the colour of innocency), being thick covered with snow. So went the white King to his grave, in the forty-eighth year of his age and the twenty-second year and tenth month of his reign (195)." *The King's funeral*

Epilogue

Charles's courage

THE COURAGE displayed by Charles during his trial and execution was widely praised. In his funeral sermon on the death of Queen Henrietta Maria many years later in 1670, the great French preacher Jacques Bénigné Bossuet, said: "I am scarce able to contemplate the greatness of his courage in those last trials; but assuredly he plainly evidenced that it is not in the power of rebels to make a king who knows himself lose his majesty (196)."

Andrew Marvell

Andrew Marvell, the Puritan poet, composed these well-known lines (197):

> *He nothing common did or mean*
> *Upon that memorable scene,*
> *But with his keener eye*
> *The axe's edge did try;*
> *Nor called the gods with vulgar spite*
> *To vindicate his helpless right,*
> *But bowed his comely head*
> *Down, as upon a bed.*

General Fairfax

General Fairfax had held himself aloof from the whole affair. He relieved his feelings in less outstanding verse (198):

> *Oh, let that day from time be blotted quite,*
> *And let belief of't in next age be waved.*
> *In deepest silence th'act concealed might,*
> *So that the Kingdom's credit might be saved.*
> *But if the Power Divine permitted this,*
> *His Will's the law and ours must acquiesce.*

Charles on the scaffold

Charles, Prince of Wales, eldest son of the executed king, who succeeded
to his father's throne as Charles II in 1660

Royalists were deeply shocked by the King's death. One of them wrote: "None of the Kings, no not one . . . ever left the world with more sorrow. Women miscarried, men fell into melancholy, some with consternations expired. Men, women and children then, and yet unborn, suffering in him and for him . . . (199)"

Royalist shock

Indeed, the consternation was general. A Yorkshire Puritan wrote: "There was such a consternation among the common people throughout the nation, that one neighbour durst scarcely speak to another when they met in the streets, not from any abhorrence at the action, but in surprise at the rarity and infrequency of it (200)."

General consternation

The most common feeling was one of stunned amazement. People went about their usual business with a quiet sense of shock. A foreign ambassador noted with surprise: "There was no disturbance in London on the day of the execution; all the shops were open in the usual way (201)."

Stunned amazement

Yet there was deep and genuine grief, too, which the newspapers were allowed to express sympathetically. Richard Collings wrote in *The Kingdom's Weekly Intelligencer*: "This Day it did not rain at all, yet it was a very wet day in and about the City of London by reason of the abundance of affliction that fell from many eyes (202)."

Deep grief

The execution of Charles was intended to abolish the monarchy as well. In March, 1649, the Rump passed an Act Abolishing the Office of King: "That the office of a King in this nation shall not henceforth reside in or be exercised by any one single person; and that no one person whatsoever shall or may have, or hold the office, style, dignity, power, or authority of King of the said kingdoms and dominions, or any of them, or of the Prince of Wales, any law, statute, usage, or custom to the contrary thereof in any wise notwithstanding (203)."

The monarchy abolished

And in an Act Establishing a Council of State, passed in the same year, the first instruction to the newly-appointed councillors was this: "You are hereby authorized and required to oppose and suppress whomsoever shall [support] the pretended title of Charles Stuart, eldest son to the late King, or any other of the said late King's issue, or claiming under him or them; or the

No more kings

The burial of Charles I at Windsor

pretended title or claim of any other single person whomsoever to the crown of England or Ireland, dominion of Wales, or to any of the dominions or territories to them or either of them belonging (204)."

Enduring words This was not to be. The Stuart monarchy was restored in 1660, when the dead King's son came to the throne as Charles II, but the trial and execution of a monarch had left a permanent mark on English history. The government of the country could never be the same again; the ideas which had defeated Charles lived on.

The words of John Cook, the King's prosecutor, written to his

wife shortly before his execution as a Regicide, were of lasting importance: "We are not traitors, nor murderers, nor fanatics, but true Christians and good Commonwealth men, fixed and constant to the principles of sanctity, truth, justice and mercy, which the Parliament and Army declared and engaged for; and to that noble principle of preferring the universality, before a particularity, that we sought the public good and would have enfranchised the people, and secured the welfare of the whole groaning creation, if the nation had not more delighted in servitude than in freedom (205)."

Some Important Dates

24th March, 1603. Death of Elizabeth I; accession of James I.

19th April, 1603. Millenary Petition presented to James I.

14th–18th January, 1604. Hampton Court Conference.

20th June, 1604. Apology of the House of Commons.

23rd June to 3rd July, 1610. Debate on Impositions.

29th August, 1611. Court of High Commission strengthened.

27th March, 1625. Death of James I; accession of Charles I.

2nd March, 1629. Parliament dissolved, having voted the Three Resolutions.

6th August, 1633. William Laud appointed Archbishop of Canterbury.

7th February, 1637. Judges decide in favour of the King in the Ship Money Case.

23rd July, 1637. Prayer Book riots in Scotland.

18th June, 1639. Charles I forced to make truce with the Scots.

13th April to 5th May, 1640. Short Parliament.

28th August, 1640. Charles again defeated by Scots.

3rd November, 1640. Long Parliament summoned.

11th December, 1640. Root and Branch Petition presented.

12th May, 1641. Thomas Wentworth, Earl of Strafford, executed.

22nd November, 1641. The Grand Remonstrance.

4th January, 1642. Charles I attempted to arrest the Five Members.

5th March, 1642. Militia Ordinance to raise an army for Ireland.

22nd August, 1642. Royal standard raised at Nottingham.

23rd October, 1642. Battle of Edgehill.

25th September, 1643. Solemn League and Covenant.

2nd July, 1644. Battle of Marston Moor.

14th June, 1645. Battle of Naseby.

5th May, 1646. Charles surrendered to the Scottish Army at Newark.

13th July, 1646. Propositions of Newcastle are sent to Charles.

1st August, 1646. Charles I answers the Propositions.

3rd February, 1647. Charles is handed over to the English Parliament by the Scots.

4th June, 1647. Charles is taken by Army to Newmarket.

1st August, 1647. Heads of the Proposals are presented to Charles.

24th August, 1647. Charles is taken to Hampton Court.

14th September, 1647. Charles I answers the Proposals.

28th October to 11th November, 1647. The Putney Debates.

11th November, 1647. Charles escapes to the Isle of Wight.

26th December, 1647. The Engagement between the King and the Scots.

17th January, 1648. Parliament makes its "Vote of No Addresses".

6th April, 1648. Charles tries to escape from Carisbrook Castle.

1st May, 1648. The Windsor Prayer-Meeting.

26th August, 1648. Surrender of Colchester.

18th September to 28th November, 1648. Newport negotiations between Charles and Parliament.

18th November, 1648. Remonstrance of the Army.

30th November, 1648. Charles is removed to Hurst Castle.

6th December, 1648. Colonel Pride's Purge of the House of Commons.

15th December, 1648. Charles is taken to Windsor.

6th January, 1649. An act is passed to create a special court for the King's Trial.

19th January, 1649. Charles is brought to London.

20th January, 1649. Agreement of the People is presented to Parliament.

20th to 27th January, 1649. The trial of Charles I.

29th January, 1649. Death Warrant issued.

30th January, 1649. Charles I beheaded outside Whitehall Palace.

9th February, 1649. Charles I is buried at Windsor.

17th March, 1649. The monarchy is abolished by Act of Parliament.

Further Reading

An excellent text of the King's trial may be found in the *Trial of Charles I*, edited by Roger Lockyer (Folio Society, London, 1959). Other collections of contemporary documents include S. R. Gardiner's *The Constitutional Documents of the Puritan Revolution* (Oxford University Press, London, 1906); J. P. Kenyon's *The Stuart Constitution* (Cambridge University Press, London, 1966); and J. R. Tanner's *Constitutional Documents of the Reign of James I* (Cambridge University Press, London, 1930).

Among contemporary works, there are the *Memoirs of the Life of Colonel Hutchinson*, written by his widow, Lucy, (Dent, London, 1965; Dutton, New York, 1965); Edward Hyde, first Earl of Clarendon, *The History of the Rebellion and Civil Wars*, ed. W. D. Macray (Oxford University Press, London, 1888; Mellifont, Wilmington, De., 1971); and Gilbert Burnet's *History of His Own Times* (Oxford University Press, London, 1897). There is also the *Eikon Basilike or The Pourtraicture of his Sacred Majestie in his Solitudes and Sufferings,* written by an unknown Royalist and published in London on the day of the King's burial (Cornell University Press, New York, 1967).

Two books which give a good account of the English background to Charles I's reign are Wallace Notestein's *The English People on the Eve of Colonization 1603–30* (Harper & Row, London and New York, 1954), and Christopher Hill's *Society and Puritanism in Pre-Revolutionary England* (Secker & Warburg, London, 1964; Schocken, New York, 1964).

Many lives have been written of the principal characters of the period. There is Evan John's *King Charles I* (Arthur Barker, London, 1952; Roy, New York, 1952), which may be supplemented by Sir Charles Petrie's *The Letters, Speeches and Proclamations of King Charles I* (Cassell, London, 1935; Funk & Wagnalls, New York, 1935). The most recent life of his chief adversary is Christopher Hill's *God's Englishman, Oliver Cromwell and the English Revolution* (Weidenfeld and Nicolson, London, 1970; The Dial Press, New York, 1970). The relationship between the two men is considered in G. M. Young's *Charles I and Cromwell* (Peter Davies, London, 1935).

Two books about the King's trial and execution are Hugh Ross Williamson's *The Day They Killed the King* (Frederick Muller, London, 1957), and C. V. Wedgwood's *The Trial of Charles I* (Collins, London, 1964; Fontana, London, 1967); and two simple accounts of the causes and consequences of the event are R. R. Sellman's *Civil War and Commonwealth* (Methuen, London, 1958), and Eleanor Murphy's *Cavaliers and Roundheads* (Longmans, London, 1965).

List of Sources

(1) C. V. Wedgwood, *The Trial of Charles I* (Collins, 1964), 9–10
(2) Gilbert Burnet, *History of His Own Times* (Everyman Ed., 1906), 15
(3) Wedgwood, *op. cit.,* 13
(4) *Ibid,* 222
(5) G. R. Elton, *The Tudor Constitution* (C.U.P., 1962), 15
(6) *Ibid,* 15
(7) *Ibid,* 15
(8) *Ibid,* 403
(9) *Ibid,* 404
(10) Lucy Hutchinson, *Memoirs of the Life of Colonel Hutchinson* (Everyman Ed., 1905), 63
(11) G. W. Prothero, *Statutes and Constitutional Documents 1558–1625* (O.U.P., 1913), 219
(12) L. W. Cowie, *The Pilgrim Fathers* (Wayland, 1970), 13
(13) C. Stephenson & F. G. Marcham, *Sources of English Constitutional History* (Harper & Brothers, 1937), 366
(14) *Ibid,* 354
(15) *Ibid,* 367
(16) *Ibid,* 375
(17) Elton, *Tudor Constitution,* 14
(18) Cowie, *op. cit.,* 18
(19) J. R. Tanner, *Constitutional Documents of the Reign of James I* (C.U.P., 1930), 15
(20) Prothero, *op. cit.,* 399
(21) Godfrey Davies, *The Early Stuarts 1603–60* (O.U.P., 1938), 31
(22) Stephenson & Marcham, *op. cit.,* 422
(23) Prothero, *op. cit.,* 413
(24) *Ibid,* 414
(25) Cowie, *Pilgrim Fathers,* 18
(26) Prothero, *op. cit.,* 67
(27) *Ibid,* 29
(28) Stephenson & Marcham, *op. cit.,* 422
(29) J. P. Kenyon, *The Stuart Constitution* (C.U.P., 1966), 183
(30) Cowie, *op. cit.,* 26
(31) Richard Baxter, *Autobiography* (Everyman Ed., 1931), 4
(32) Cowie, *op. cit.,* 16
(33) Prothero, *op. cit.,* 350
(34) Burnet, *His Own Times,* 8
(35) *Ibid,* 8
(36) G. Huehns (ed.), *Selections from Clarendon* (O.U.P., World's Classics, 1955), 68
(37) Kenyon, *Stuart Constitution,* 171
(38) I. Deane Jones, *The English Revolution 1603–1714* (Heinemann, 1931), 29
(39) Kenyon, *op. cit.,* 149
(40) Deane Jones, *op. cit.,* 47
(41) Kenyon, *op. cit.,* 85
(42) Godfrey Davies, *Early Stuarts,* 70
(43) Hugh Ross Williamson, *John Hampden* (Hodder, 1933), 208
(44) *Clarendon,* 83
(45) Edward Phillips, *Baker's Chronicle* (1670), 478
(46) *Clarendon,* 8
(47) C. H. Firth, *Oliver Cromwell* (Putnam, 1935), 50
(48) *Ibid,* 39
(49) Deane Jones, *English Revolution,* 39
(50) Sir Charles Petrie, *The Letters, Speeches and Proclamations of King Charles I* (Cassell, 1935), 115
(51) J. P. Kenyon, *The Stuart Constitution,* 173
(52) S. R. Gardiner, *Constitutional Documents of the Puritan Revolution 1625–1660* (O.U.P., 1899), 137
(53) Petrie, *op. cit.,* 117
(54) Baxter, *Autobiography,* 31
(55) *Clarendon,* 231
(56) Baxter, *op. cit.,* 32
(57) Petrie, *op. cit.,* 117
(58) Deane Jones, *op. cit.,* 66
(59) Godfrey Davies, *The Early Stuarts,* 102
(60) Baxter, *op. cit.,* 34
(61) *Ibid,* 34
(62) *Ibid,* 34
(63) *Ibid,* 35
(64) Godfrey Davies, *op. cit.,* 125
(65) Lucy Hutchinson, *Colonel Hutchinson,* 78
(66) Godfrey Davies, *op.*

cit., 125

(67) *Clarendon*, 249
(68) Petrie, *op. cit.*, 136
(69) Deane Jones, *op. cit.*, 74
(70) *Ibid*, 79
(71) Charles Firth, *Cromwell*, 84
(72) Gardiner, *The Puritan Revolution*, 270
(73) H. Bettenson, *Documents of the Christian Church* (O.U.P., World's Classics, 1943), 394
(74) Petrie, *op. cit.*, 143
(75) Thomas Carlyle, *Letters and Speeches of Oliver Cromwell* (1 vol. ed., Hutchinson, 1905), 70
(76) Petrie, *op. cit.*, 174
(77) *Ibid*, 175
(78) G. M. Young, *Charles I and Cromwell* (Peter Davies, 1935), 17
(79) Petrie, *op. cit.*, 200
(80) *Ibid*, 202–3
(81) Gardiner, *op. cit.*, 307
(82) M. A. Gibb, *The Lord General* (Lindsay Drummond, 1938), 164
(83) *Ibid*, 165
(84) Young, *op. cit.*, 67
(85) Petrie, *op. cit.*, 230
(86) Gardiner, *op. cit.*, 327
(87) Godfrey Davies, *op. cit.*, 145
(88) Deane Jones, *op. cit.*, 32
(89) Gibb, *op. cit.*, 184
(90) Young, *op. cit.*, 77
(91) *Ibid*, 78
(92) Gibb, *op. cit.*, 184
(93) *Ibid*, 185
(94) *Ibid*, 185
(95) *Ibid*, 186
(96) Young, *op. cit.*, 91–2
(97) Gibb, *op. cit.*, 190

(98) Gardiner, *Puritan Revolution*, 349
(99) *Ibid*, 356
(100) Young, *op. cit.*, 102
(101) Gibb, *op. cit.*, 192
(102) Carlyle, *Cromwell's Letters & Speeches*, 127
(103) Wedgwood, *Trial of Charles I*, 12
(104) Gibb, *op. cit.*, 201
(105) Young, *op. cit.*, 112
(106) Wedgwood, *op. cit.*, 29
(107) Young, *op. cit.*, 129–30
(108) Wedgwood, *op. cit.*, 30
(109) *Ibid*, 31
(110) Firth, *Cromwell*, 30
(111) Wedgwood, *op. cit.*, 33
(112) *Ibid*, 37
(113) *Ibid*, 32
(114) Gibb, *Lord General*, 209
(115) *Ibid*, 210
(116) *Ibid*, 211
(117) Firth, *op. cit.*, 216
(118) Wedgwood, *op. cit.*, 63
(119) *Ibid*, 45
(120) Gardiner, *op. cit.*, 357–8
(121) *Clarendon*, 310
(122) *Ibid*, 310
(123) *Ibid*, 311
(124) Gardiner, *op. cit.*, 370
(125) Firth, *op. cit.*, 218
(126) *Ibid*, 218
(127) *Clarendon*, 34
(128) to (137); (143) to (165); (167) to (174) Roger Lockyer, *The Trial of Charles I* (Folio Society, 1959) contains the text of the King's trial; and it may also be found in Petrie, *Letters of Charles I*, 243–261
(138) *Clarendon*, 315
(139) Gardiner, *op. cit.*, 374
(140) *Ibid*, 375
(141) *Ibid*, 375
(142) *Ibid*, 376
(143) to (165) Lockyer, *op. cit.*

(166) *Clarendon*, 314
(167) to (174) Lockyer, *op. cit.*
(175) Wedgwood, *op. cit.*, 166
(176) Gardiner, *op. cit.*, 386
(177) Wedgwood, *op. cit.*, 178
(178) *Ibid*, 167
(179) *Ibid*, 168
(180) *Ibid*, 169
(181) Young, *op. cit.*, 168
(182) *Ibid*, 169
(183) Wedgwood, *op. cit.*, 180
(184) Gibb, *op. cit.*, 215
(185) Wedgwood, *op. cit.*, 189–90
(186) *Ibid*, 190
(187) *Ibid*, 191
(188) *Ibid*, 191–92
(189) *Ibid*, 192
(190) *Ibid*, 192
(191) *Ibid*, 193
(192) Firth, *Cromwell*, 229
(193) Burnet, *His Own Times*, 15
(194) Hugh Ross Williamson, *The Day They Killed the King* (Muller, 1957), 147
(195) John Buchan, *Oliver Cromwell* (Reprint Society, 1941), 266
(196) *Ibid*, 266
(197) *Horation Ode upon Cromwell's Return from Ireland*
(198) Gibb, *op. cit.*, 216
(199) Wedgwood, *op. cit.*, 196
(200) *Ibid*, 196
(201) Gibb, *op. cit.*, 216
(202) Wedgwood, *op. cit.*, 197
(203) Gardiner, *op. cit.*, 386
(204) Stephenson & Marcham, *op. cit.*, 519
(205) Wedgwood, *op. cit.*, 221

Picture Credits

Index

127